20 Classroom
•Stories •Activities •Prayer Services

Stacy Schumacher & Jim Fanning

TWENTY-THIRD PUBLICATIONS
Mystic, Connecticut 06355

**Illustrations by
Dorry Clay**

**Mechanical illustrations by
William Baker**

Twenty-Third Publications
185 Willow Street
P.O. Box 180
Mystic, CT 06355
(203) 536-2611
800-321-0411

© Copyright 1994 Stacy Schumacher and Jim Fanning. All rights reserved.
The prayer services work best when each participant has a copy, so permission is granted to duplicate them, as needed, for non-commercial use in schools, churches, and for other prayer groups. The section "Taking the Message Home" may also be duplicated. Otherwise, no part of this publication may be reproduced in any manner without prior written permission of the publisher. Write to Permissions Editor.

ISBN 0-89622-611-5
Library of Congress Catalog Card Number 94-60479
Printed in the U.S.A.

"An excellent collection of ideas, activities, and stories that have the unique potential of relating to all celebrations, to the Author of Life. This practical resource will be a great help to all charged with the task of leading children to find God in all of life. Celebration is at the heart of our Christian story and tradition, and *Celebrating Holidays* creatively restores this very important dimension of the human story. Stacy Schumacher and Jim Fanning have gifted us with the possibilities of reclaiming our religious holidays, while adding a spiritual dimension to our secular celebrations."

Sr. Edith Prendergast, R.S.C.
Director of Religious Education
Archdiocese of Los Angeles

"Religious education coordinators and teachers are always looking for fresh and useful material. Stacy Schumacher and Jim Fanning's book offers sometimes good, sometimes very good, but always practical suggestions. I recommend it."

Rev. Joseph M. Champlin
Pastor, Lecturer, and Author of 37 books

"Reading *Celebrating Holidays* is a treat. Schumacher and Fanning have put together twenty celebrations that children and teachers are sure to enjoy. I especially like the way the prayer services use concrete images from children's experiences and how the take-home activities provide specific suggestions for living out the lesson throughout the week.

"This is a joyful guide for helping children and teachers become aware of and celebrate God in their midst throughout the year and a great way to pep up any curriculum!"

Carole MacClennan
Author, *Learning By Doing*

"This book of celebrations is a splendid resource for helping teachers and children commemorate holidays that all of us love. It is easy-to-use, creative, practical, and filled with values that we hope children will associate with and own as part of their enjoyment of these annual occasions. I strongly recommend it not only for teachers but also for parents who like to read stories to their children and pray with them as part of a holiday's ritual."

Janaan Manternach
Co-author with Carl J. Pfeifer of *This is Our Faith* series and *Creative Catechist*

"This book will help families and youth find a sense of the sacred in the ordinary experiences of life. With stories, reflection, scripture and prayer, home activities, and discussion starters, it is a user-friendly resource for anyone interested in getting young people to see the connection between faith and life.

"This is one of the best family-centered books I have seen in a long time. If a family uses this, there will be no vacation from God during the summer months. It also will be useful in school and religious education programs."

Fr. Joseph Felker, Pastor
Redlands, California

Contents

	Introduction	*1*
1	*Labor Day* *Blessing Our Work*	*2*
2	*The First Day of Fall* *A Time of Change*	*8*
3	*Columbus Day* *A Time for Discovery*	*14*
4	*Halloween* *A Not Too Scary Celebration*	*20*
5	*Thanksgiving* *A Time for Gratitude*	*26*
6	*St. Nicholas Day* *A Christmas Saint*	*32*
7	*Christmas* *A Season for Jesus*	*38*
8	*New Year's Day* *A New Beginning*	*45*
9	*Martin Luther King Day* *Dreaming of a Better World*	*51*
10	*Valentine's Day* *Love One Another*	*57*

11	*Presidents' Day* Who Shall Lead Us?	63
12	*Mardi Gras* Leading to Lent	70
13	*St. Patrick's Day* What's Behind the 'Wearin' of the Green?	76
14	*First Day of Spring* Signs of New Life	82
15	*April Fool's Day* A Time for Laughter	87
16	*Earth Day* Treasuring Our Planet	93
17	*Mother's Day* Thank God for Mothers	98
18	*Last Day of School* A Time of Re-Creation	103
19	*Father's Day* Thank God for Fathers	109
20	*The Fourth of July* Celebrating Freedom	116
	Puzzle Solutions	123

Introduction

Children love a holiday. They love the preparations; they love the anticipation; they love the decorations, the traditions, the rituals, the break in their routines. Finally, they love the day itself—the celebration! So many elements of holiday observance have parallels in church practices, it seems that religion teachers are really missing an important opportunity if they don't tap into the children's enthusiasm to make religious connections.

In fact, many of the holidays that children love so much have roots in religious celebrations or observances. Some of these, like Halloween, have been taken over by secular trappings. Others, such as Christmas, still have religious content, but are in the process of being usurped by the world. Still other festive days, such as Martin Luther King Day and Earth Day, have no religious background but relate well to spiritual themes. All of life's celebrations can be related to the Author of life.

That is the intention of *Celebrating Holidays*: to reclaim the religious holidays for our children and to add a spiritual dimension to secular celebrations. In this way we hope to make what is important in the youngster's life a "teachable moment" to bring them closer to God.

Each holiday unit contains five features: a story, discussion questions, a craft or activity, a prayer service, and a page to take home and live out during the days ahead. Catechists could use one chapter as an entire lesson or use one or two ideas from an appropriate chapter to enrich a lesson.

The celebrations in this book call for the involvement of many individuals. To facilitate their participation, the pages may be duplicated, including the prayer services, the activities, and "Taking the Message Home."

However one makes use of the ideas about the holidays in this book of celebrations, do so with wonder, delight, and joyous celebration. The children will understand the holiday better and be enriched by it not only this year, but every year when the special day recurs.

Labor Day
Blessing Our Work

Work, even school work, is good and can be fun. What a wonderful message to give children as they begin a new school year! Although Labor Day honors everyone who works—and that's most of us, even children!—this unique holiday usually doesn't remind us of labor at all. Rather, it simply and depressingly represents the end of summer and the return to school. Even though classes often start after Labor Day, it's still a good idea to celebrate after the fact God's gift of work with our youngsters.

Benjamin's Friend

Scuffing his sandals through the dusty street, Benjamin tossed his new wooden ball into the air. The wood made a satisfying smack on his hands as he caught the spinning sphere. The ball was a birthday gift from his parents. Birthday presents were not common among Benjamin's people, but he was a first-born son and so was especially honored.

Benjamin hurried toward a small one-story house under a palm tree where his best friend lived. He could smell bread baking and he was drawn by the tantalizing smell. No one in the village baked bread as delicious as Jesse's mother's.

Benjamin ran to the back of the house looking for his friend, anxious to show him his new toy. Hitting a ball with a stick was considered great sport among the neighborhood boys and girls, and Jesse was particularly good at it.

But Jesse was hard at work, sanding a large piece of wood. The clean smell of freshly cut lumber was in the air, and sawdust mingled with the sand on the ground. "Look at my new ball, Jesse," Benjamin shouted, "Come on and play! If you hit the ball, I'll chase it!"

Jesse looked up from his work. "Sounds like fun, Benjy, but I can't right now. I'm helping my father with his work." Benjamin was disappointed.

"Work? Who wants to do that? Come and play with me—your father will never know you're gone."

Jesse laughed. "He'll know when he comes back from the market and this wood is left undone."

Benjamin frowned. "I hate work, it's stupid. It always gets in the way of having fun."

"I don't think your new ball is stupid," said Jesse.

"My ball? What's that got to do with it?"

"My father made your ball, and he worked hard to get it just right."

"He did?" Benjamin was surprised. He had never thought about who had made the ball or about work having anything to do with fun.

"My father says that work is a gift blessed by God," Jesse replied, "and by doing our work well we in turn praise and bless God."

"I guess that's true," admitted Benjamin, who remembered the rabbi saying the same thing. "Your father knows a lot. Even my dad thinks so. He says, 'Joseph should have been a rabbi, not a carpenter.'"

"God has blessed me with a wonderful father," said Jesse. He looked so serious that Benjamin laughingly called him by his full name.

"Well, Jesus, son of Joseph, how long will it take you to finish your father's work?"

"A lifetime," laughed Jesse. "But I'll finish this job a lot faster if you'll help me. Then we can play with your new ball."

(Tradition tells us that Jesus grew up to become a carpenter himself, and he worked at that craft until he began his public ministry of teaching and healing at about age 30. The church honors Joseph, the foster father of Jesus, as the patron saint of all workers.)

Talking It Over

1. Benjamin was surprised that work could lead to fun. Can you think of ways that work can be fun?

2. Have you ever wanted to play when it was time to work? How did you feel? Would you have felt better if you remembered that God blesses your work?

3. What sort of work are you asked to do? How does doing your work well "bless," or benefit, you? How does it "bless" others? How does it praise God?

Activity—Praise Pennants

Pennants celebrating the work of our hands can add to the festivity of the prayer service, besides being fun to make.

Materials needed: triangular pieces cut from 8 1/2" x 11" paper; markers or crayons; thin dowels or plastic straws; tempera paint in shallow dishes; staplers.

Have the children write a slogan or saying on one side of the paper with markers or crayons. For example, "Lord, bless our work," "Our hands praise you," or "Bless the work of our hands." On the other side have them make a hand print with tempera paint. (Applying paint to each child's hand with a brush is slightly less messy, if somewhat less fun, than dipping them in the dish of paint.) When these papers have dried, staple to the top third of a drinking straw or glue to a wooden dowel. In the prayer service, have them wave the pennants as they pray: "Lord, bless the work of our hands."

Prayer Service—Human Creativity

Opening Song: "God Is Building a House" by Carey Landry.

Leader God, you created the world and everything in it. You give us work to do and you help us to do it. Help us to understand our work as a special gift from you that re-creates your world. We make this prayer through Jesus, your son and our brother.

All Amen.

Reader 1	Let us pray Psalm 90 together. The response is: "Lord, bless the work of our hands."
Reader 2	Before the mountains were made, and the world was brought forth, from forever to forever you are God.
All	Lord, bless the work of our hands.
Reader 3	Teach us to live our days in a right way, that we may gain wisdom of heart.
All	Lord, bless the work of our hands.
Reader 4	Fill us at dawn with your kindness, that we may shout for joy and gladness all our life.
All	Lord, bless the work of our hands.
Reader 5	Let your work be seen by us, your servants, and let your glory be seen by generations to come.
All	Lord, bless the work of our hands.
Leader	God is a good worker! •Can you think of ways in which God is working right now? (cares for us, listens to our prayers) •At the beginning of the Bible, in the book of Genesis, we read a story about God working very hard. Do you know what story that is? (the story of creation) •What work was God doing? (creating the world) •Can you name some things God made? What was God's best piece of work? (human beings) •How did God feel about this work? (God found it to be good) •We know that everything God created is very good. The really exciting thing is that God calls us to share in this good work. Can you think of ways in which you help God to re-create? (protect Earth's environment, love one another, help our families) God calls each of us to special kinds of work, and gives each of us special gifts so that we can do a good job. Let's listen now to the words of Saint Paul as he talks about work.
Reader 1	A reading from the first letter of Paul to the Corinthians (12:4–11, adapted) There are many different kinds of gifts, but the same Spirit gives

them all. There are different ways of serving, but all serve the same Lord. There are different kinds of work, but the same God works in all. The Spirit's presence is seen in each person for the good of all people.

Reader 2 The Spirit gives one person the ability to speak with wisdom. Another person receives from the same Spirit a talent for teaching. From the one Spirit, someone is given faith, while another receives the power to heal.

Reader 3 Another is able to work miracles, while still another is a prophet. One can tell the difference between what is good and what is evil; another speaks in tongues; while another interprets what has been said.

Reader 4 But all of this is the work of the one and only Spirit, who gives to each person a different gift.
The Word of the Lord.

All Thanks be to God.

Leader Please repeat after me:

Creator God,
you worked to form this world
in all its colorful wonder.
Help us to share
in your work of creation
and to use the gifts you've given us
to do the good work
you call us to do.
Bless all that we do in our work,
in the name of Jesus. Amen.

Taking the Message Home

This week see how often you can do your chores without grumbling. You might even try to offer to do a job around the house without being asked. The more you practice being a cheerful worker, the easier it will be. It might be helpful to remember that God blesses you in your work!

Lord, Bless the Work We Do . . .

Work I Have to Do   Jobs I Offer to Do

Day 1 _____   _____

2 _____   _____

3 _____   _____

4 _____   _____

5 _____   _____

6 _____   _____

7 _____   _____

Give yourself a smile face each time you do a job cheerfully.

Give yourself a star each time you offer to do a job at home or school.

2
The First Day of Fall
A Time of Change

Fall is an exciting, challenging, and sometimes difficult time of change for students. They face new teachers, friends, books, classes—perhaps even new schools! Catechists can help children experience God's presence in this time of transition by exploring God's gift of change.

A Change for Marilee

Head down, chin trembling, Marilee kicked at the fallen leaves as she cut through the park on her way home from school. "Why do people say they have a broken heart when they feel sad?" she wondered. "I feel like I have a 'broken stomach.'" Since the night before, when her mother and father told her they were getting a divorce, her stomach had had a giant lump in it. It felt like someone had kicked her.

"Nothing will ever be the same," she thought. "Dad won't be

around to help me practice softball. Christmas will be ruined. My friends will laugh at me. We'll never sit around after dinner playing Trivial Pursuit again."

As she thought of one terrible thing after another, tears started rolling down Marilee's face once again. She had been crying all day, whenever no one else was around.

Not watching where she was going, Marilee almost ran into someone coming across the park. "Oops," said Maria Chavez, a friend of her parents who lived three houses from Marilee, "You almost ran right over me!" Noticing Marilee's tears, Maria wrapped her arms around her. "Honey, what's the matter?" she asked.

"Oh, Maria, everything's the matter!" Marilee burst out. "My parents are getting a divorce and my life is ruined."

"Come on, let's sit down a minute and you can tell me about it," said Maria.

Sitting on a park bench, Marilee told Maria about last night's conversation. She explained that her father was moving to an apartment this very weekend and that she'd hardly ever see him again.

Maria listened quietly while Marilee poured out her story. Then she said, "Marilee, you must have had some idea that your parents were having problems."

"Well, yes," admitted Marilee, "they have been fighting a lot. Sometimes I'd hear them when they thought I was sleeping. And my Mom has been looking pretty sad lately. My Dad has been real quiet, not as funny and silly as he usually is."

"Marilee," Maria said, "sometimes married people just can't work things out to live happily together. If both of them are miserable, they make everyone around them unhappy too. Your parents have probably given this a lot of thought and they must think that divorce would be better for all of you."

"How can you say that?" yelled Marilee. "It's going to be awful. Our family is destroyed!"

Maria looked at her friend. "Remember last summer when you were so worried about changing from your old school? What happened when you started at your new middle school in the fall?"

"Well," Marilee said slowly, "At first it was awful. I didn't know where to go or what to do. But after a while I got used to everything and made new friends."

"And isn't it better than your old school?"

"Oh, yes!" smiled Marilee, her first real smile that day. "I can do a lot more on my own; I feel more grown up."

"That's the way change is," nodded Maria. "It's often painful but it makes us grow."

"You mean that if I wait for the pain to pass," Marilee said, wiping away her tears, "things might even be better than before?"

"Honey," smiled Maria, hugging Marilee, "Change is really a part of life, and it can be beautiful. Look at these autumn leaves, a sign of the changing seasons. Aren't they gorgeous? Now let's see how many colors we can spot on our way home for some hot apple cider."

Talking It Over

1. Marilee was facing a difficult change because of her parents' divorce. Have you ever experienced a difficult change? How did you make it through the change? (prayer, talking, finding information, etc.) Did the change lead to something good?

2. Read a Gospel story about change, for example, the Annunciation (Luke 1:26–30); or meeting the risen Christ (Luke 24:13–35). How did God work through change in these stories? How did the people in the stories change?

3. Since change is a natural part of life, it is important to be open to it. What are some ways you can be more open to change?

Activity—Circle of Change

A fall wreath can remind us of God's presence during times of change.

Materials needed: paper plate for each child; a hole punch; glue; red, orange (or yellow) yarn (ribbon of these colors, optional); a collection of fall leaves and seed pods. (If gathering these is a chore, add lentils or split peas to "fill in" the wreaths.)

To prepare for this craft, cut the center out of the plates for a more "professional" looking finished wreath.

Punch 2 holes in the top of each plate two to three inches apart. Cut yarn into 12" strips, and, if desired, cut ribbon into 12" lengths. (If your group is young, tie the ribbon into bows.)

When your group is ready, give the children the plates, and have them spread glue over the entire circle liberally. Then have them glue the fall leaves and seed pods to the outer edges. Add a bow at the top or bottom, if desired, and tie yarn through the holes for hanging.

Prayer Service—Fall

Opening Song: "The Butterfly Song" by Mary Lu Walker (Paulist Press), or "Signs of New Life" by Carey Landry (NALR), or another suitable song.

Leader   Heavenly Father, we watch the changes you send in the fall: leaves turning colors, orange and red berries on bushes, days getting shorter and cooler. Help us to enjoy the wonderful changes that you give us to make life interesting. When changes come that are hard for us, help us to remember that you are with us. Remind us that you always give us chances to grow into stronger, more loving people when changes come into our lives. We make this prayer in the name of Jesus our Lord.

All	Amen.
Reader 1	Let us ask our Father in heaven to forgive us for the times we blamed others for changes that they couldn't do anything about, Lord, have mercy . . .
All	Lord, have mercy.
Reader 2	For the times we made things harder for people, like substitute teachers, who were new to us, Christ, have mercy . . .
All	Christ, have mercy.
Reader 1	For the times we didn't make the best of things when changes came that we didn't like, Lord, have mercy . . .
All	Lord, have mercy.
Reader 2	Father, you gave us a world that is always changing. Help us to see your loving hand guiding us when changes make us afraid, and forgive us when we forget to count on you.
All	Amen.

(Tell or read together the story of Abraham and his journey to a new home. See Genesis 12:1–5,7,9,10; 13:1–6,8–9,11–12,14–18.)

Leader	This reading tells the story of Abraham. He had a good life and didn't need to change anything about it in order to be happy. He had a very beautiful wife and lots of land, servants, and cattle. But one day God told him to pack up and move. Abraham didn't argue. He didn't ask why the new place would be better, or what he would gain by moving. He just did it. Abraham trusted that God would help him with any problems that would come up during his travels—and plenty did! God stayed with Abraham and rewarded him for his great faith by making him the father of the Israelites. Even today, Christians, Muslims, and Jews remember Abraham as the "father of faith." Spend a moment in silence now to ask God to give you strong faith such as Abraham had. (Allow two minutes for this.)
Leader	Repeat after me: Father in heaven, give us strong faith. Help us to trust you completely

as Abraham did.
Help us to know
that you are with us always
as you were with Abraham.
We ask this through our Lord Jesus Christ,
who lives and reigns with you for ever and ever. Amen.

Taking the Message Home

Looking for Changes

Make a list of changes you notice around you—in nature or people. Try to write something good that could come from this change. One is already done for you.

CHANGE	GOOD RESULT
Leaves die	beautiful colors

Reprinted with permission from *Celebrating Holidays* by Stacy Schumacher and Jim Fanning
© 1994 Twenty-Third Publications, P.O. Box 180, Mystic, CT 06355. 800-321-0411

3
Columbus Day
A Time for Discovery

All children know that Columbus discovered America. For many students, Columbus Day is a school holiday, so it must be important! For religion teachers, it can be a prime time to help our students see God's work in the immense variety of our world. Columbus's courage and faith carried him on a voyage of discovery. With courage and faith, we can be open to discover, and appreciate, the differences we encounter in people, customs, and places.

Angelo's Voyage of Discovery

All was dark and silent as the three small ships sailed through unknown waters. Angelo, the cabin boy on the Pinta, yawned and pulled his coat tighter against the cold.

"Thirty-seven days," sighed Angelo, looking down into the deep, dark water. "Thirty-seven days we've been sailing and still no sign of land." Angelo peered back into the blackness of the night. No sign of the other vessels, the Niña or the Santa Maria. Captain Columbus was aboard the Santa Maria, leading this expedition in search of the gold and treasures of the Orient.

"But," thought Angelo, glumly leaning against the rail, "now no one knows where we are, not even Captain Columbus." Many thought Columbus was insane, a dreamer who believed the world was round, and who further believed he could reach the Orient by sailing west, a direct route.

"Now even the crew thinks he's crazy," Angelo said to himself, grimly remembering the angry whispers of the sailors, plotting when and how they would take over the ships and turn them back to Spain. Angelo couldn't help smiling as he recalled the times he, too, had felt like pushing Captain Columbus overboard! "Is all this anger, fear, and growing hatred worth the riches of the Indies?" he wondered.

Surprised by a sudden presence beside him, Angelo turned to see one of the ship's cats (brought along to catch the rats aboard) brushing against his legs. Angelo picked up his purring friend and held her warm fur against his cheek. He remembered that this voyage was about more than treasure. Each night Captain Columbus led his men in prayer. He planned on sharing the Gospel with the peoples they would meet. And Angelo knew it took great faith to keep issuing the command "Forward," even when faced with the unknown.

Suddenly both the cat and the boy jumped at the booming voice of the Pinta's cannon. "That is the signal for land!" Angelo realized. "Could it be true?" Then he heard another sound, a voice calling out, "Land ho!"

It was really true, land at last! Now the crew was running up onto the deck, some were shouting, some had fallen to their knees, some were even crying. But Angelo just hugged his cat even tighter as he quietly gave thanks for Captain Columbus's faith and courage. Under his leadership they had reached a new land, and Angelo smiled as he thought of the new people they would soon meet. They would probably be very different from the people he knew.

"I wonder how they will look," he thought. "What kind of clothes will they wear? How will they talk? What will they think of us?" This last idea made Angelo chuckle to himself. "We might seem funnier and stranger to them than they do to us," he realized. Filled with excitement and wonder about who and what he would find on shore, Angelo thanked God for bringing them safely to this new place and for creating different lands to discover.

Talking It Over

1. Have you ever gone on a "voyage of discovery?" Was it exciting? Scary? Why? (Examples might be a field trip to something brand new, dinner at the home of a friend from a different country, or a trip to a faraway city.)

2. Columbus opened up new worlds to us. How do we treat people who are from other parts of the world? What are some ways we can appreciate the differences in others?

3. Amid the excitement of discovering land, Angelo turned to prayer. When do you like to pray? Discover new times and places to pray.

Activity—Leaf Rubbings

We discover and celebrate the wonderful variety in nature by making leaf rubbings. Materials needed: white paper; construction paper; glue; unwrapped crayons (broken pieces are okay); different kinds of leaves from house plants, trees, herbs, ferns, all kinds! (Thin leaves work best.)

Give each child a piece of white paper. They can share the leaves and crayons. Have them place one leaf at a time under the paper and then rub the side of an unwrapped crayon over it. The pattern of the leaf appears on the paper. An interesting effect can be produced by doing each leaf in a different color. After the leaves have been rubbed, the completed masterpiece can be mounted on construction paper for a "finished" look.

Prayer Service—Discovery

Opening Song: "It's A Small World" (Disneyland Records), or another suitable discovery song.

Leader Father, you have made a world of great variety: mountains, plains, hills, seas, rivers, ponds, and streams. You have given us all kinds of plants, flowers, trees, and animals. You have made us, your people, with all shades of skin—from darkest black to palest peach, and with blond, brown, gray, black, and red hair.

Yet, we are all made in your image. You love each of us and are pleased with the variety you have created. Help us to keep our eyes and hearts open to discover more about you through the wonders you have made. We ask this in the name of Jesus, our Lord.

All Amen.

Reader 1 A reading from the first letter of Paul to the Corinthians (12:12–13, 21–22, 25–31)
(after the reading) The Word of the Lord.

All Thanks be to God.

Leader God could have created a world with one kind of tree, one type of flower, one sort of scenery, and one species of animal. God could have made us all alike or very similar. What a boring world it would be! Can you imagine eating the same food not only every day, but three times every day?

Instead, there is so much variety that after thousands of years we still have not learned all there is to know about the world and its people. New things are being discovered every day. Each one of us can use our special gifts to discover things we never knew, and perhaps some of us will make discoveries never before made!

Litany of Praise

(All respond: We praise you, Lord. If possible, have the children make this response in a foreign language. See samples below.)

Reader 2	That we will discover you in each other, we pray . . .
All	We praise you, Lord.
Reader 3	For eyes that are blue, brown, gray, or green, we pray . . .
All	We praise you, Lord.
Reader 4	For pizza, tacos, spaghetti, egg rolls, hamburgers, and fried chicken, we pray . . .
All	We praise you, Lord.
Reader 5	For voices, high and deep, soft and loud, young and old, we pray . . .
All	We praise you, Lord.
Reader 6	For babies, toddlers, children, teens, adults, the elderly, we pray . . .
All	We praise you, Lord.
Reader 7	For your abundant gifts, including laughter, music, creativity, friendship, and love, we pray . . .
All	We praise you, Lord.
Reader 8	For the languages in which we can sing your praises, we pray . . .
All	We praise you, Lord.
Leader	Loving Father, you created the world and everything in it. You formed all nations and made people with unique gifts and qualities. Guide us on our voyage of discovery as we learn to value the ex-

citing differences in our neighborhoods, schools, in our country, and in our world. We pray in the name of Jesus, the Lord. Amen.

Egyptian:	Ehna be te solee ashen enta, Ya Sur.
German:	Wir loben dich, Herr.
Spanish:	Te alabamos, Señor.
Italian:	Glorificamo a Signore.
French:	Glorifions le Seigneur.
Tagalog:	Pinupuri ka namin, panginoon Diyos.

Taking the Message Home

Discovering Our Heritage

This week talk to your Mom, Dad, aunt, uncle, or grandparents about your family heritage. Ask them these questions and try to discover who you are and where you came from.

- What country (countries) did your ancestors come from?

- Where were your parents born?

- Where were your grandparents born?

- Where were your great-grandparents born?

- Where did they first live when they came to America?

- What language did they speak?

- What kind of work did they do?

Be proud of your background, whatever it is! It has helped make you who and what you are today, unique, special, and different from all others!

Reprinted with permission from *Celebrating Holidays* by Stacy Schumacher and Jim Fanning
1994 Twenty-Third Publications, P.O. Box 180, Mystic, CT 06355. 800-321-0411

4

Halloween
A Not Too Scary Celebration

Nasty "tricks" have diminished the fun and innocence of Halloween for some adults, but this unique holiday remains a glorious one-of-a-kind celebration for children. Religion teachers can use this time of fun and delicious scariness to examine the Christian meaning behind the many symbols of Halloween.

A Night to Remember

"What do you think of this face?" Sharlene asked her uncle Doug, pushing her crayon drawing of a jack-o-lantern across the table.

Uncle Doug looked up from the pumpkin he was cutting open. "It's a funny face."

"It's supposed to be scary," said Sharlene, disappointed.

"Oh, the drawing," said Uncle Doug, slapping his hand to his head. "I thought you meant your face."

Sharlene giggled. She liked having Uncle Doug at her house

after school until her mother came home from work. He was always ready to play a game or help Sharlene and her twin brother, Steve, with their homework. This day was extra special because it was Halloween, and Uncle Doug was helping Steve and Sharlene with all the last-minute touches.

"There you are, Steve," said Uncle Doug as Sharlene's twin came into the dining room. "You'd better get started taking the glop out of the pumpkin so I can carve out the face Sharlene has designed for us. And I can't wait to see your costume. The neighbors are still talking about last year when you were the human computer."

"This is a nice big pumpkin," approved Sharlene, "but why do we carve faces into pumpkins for Halloween?"

"And then put lighted candles inside," said Steve, his fingers full of squishy pumpkin. "How come?"

"It's a very old tradition," answered Uncle Doug, "just as Halloween is a very old holiday. Almost everything about Halloween has something to do with being a Christian, because Halloween has Christian origins."

"It does?" asked Sharlene in surprise.

"Think." Uncle Doug went on, "What special thing will we do tomorrow—besides eat candy?"

"Well," said Steve thoughtfully, "we'll go to Mass because it's a holy day."

"That's right," nodded Sharlene. "All Saints Day."

"And the saints are holy, right?" Uncle Doug continued. "And 'hallow' is another word for 'holy.' Think of the Our Father: 'Hallowed be thy name.' So if tomorrow is All Hallow's Day, then tonight is . . ."

"All Hallow's Eve!" said the twins.

"And those words kind of came together to become Halloween," smiled Uncle Doug.

"But how did Halloween get to be scary?" they asked.

"Long ago, the Celts in England and Ireland celebrated New Year's Day on November 1, so October 31 was an end-of-the-year celebration. On that day, they remembered all those who died during the past year, and they believed that on that night the dead came back to be with the living. The villagers wore masks and costumes to disguise themselves as ghosts and led the real ghosts out of town with a parade."

"That sounds kind of Halloweeny," said Steve, "but I still don't see why it's Christian."

"It wasn't, until Christians spread the idea that, thanks to Jesus' resurrection, we no longer had to fear death or any kind of evil—so we could even dress up and make fun of death and the things that represent it."

"Like skeletons!" shouted Steve.

"But what about witches," asked Sharlene, "and bats and owls and black cats?"

"Those are things associated with evil, or maybe just things that scare us," Uncle Doug explained. "But we never have to be afraid of anything, because Jesus is always with us. In the eighth century when Pope Gregory III changed the feast of All Saints to November 1, the focus of the night before really began to change."

"Well, I know one thing that doesn't have anything to do with our faith," Steve said, his mouth full of donut. "Trick-or-treating!"

"Don't be so sure," laughed Uncle Doug. "The Celts fed costumed people who came to their door on Halloween because they might really be ghosts. But later, Christian children would go door-to-door offering prayers for the dead in exchange for food. They'd ask for 'soul cakes.' Then one Halloween, a cook cut a hole in the traditional soul cake dough, popped it in hot fat, and invented the donut. And since the donut has no beginning or end, it's a reminder of eternal life."

"But you still haven't explained the jack-o-lantern," said Sharlene.

"Saved the best for last," Uncle Doug smiled as he began carving the pumpkin. "Travelers who had to go a long distance to Mass for All Saints Day would stop at Christian homes along the way. People would put a candle in the window as a sign that travelers were welcome. Since it was fall and the autumn wind might blow out the flame, they carved out a pumpkin or squash in which to protect it."

"Wow!" said Sharlene, "I never knew Halloween had so much to do with being a Catholic! I'll have to tell Mom all about it when we go trick-or-treating tonight."

"And it's given me an idea for a costume," said Steve, washing down his third donut with cider. "Since Halloween is on the eve of All Saints, I'm going to dress up as one of the saints!"

"You, a saint?" laughed Uncle Doug, giving both Steve and Sharlene a hug. "The neighbors will never believe it!"

Talking It Over

1. What Halloween explanations or traditions do you think are most interesting or surprising?

2. Why do you think the Celts were so afraid of ghosts coming out on New Year's Eve?

3. Why do Christians have less reason to be afraid than people who don't know about Jesus?

Activity—A Halloween Mola

The *mola* is a Central American art form made by stitching bright-colored cloth symbols onto a piece of black material. A Halloween *mola* can remind children of what they have learned about some of the Halloween symbols.

Materials needed: large sheets of black construction paper; 2"-3" symbol patterns cut out of cardboard (include such shapes as pumpkins, cats, owls, candles, witch hats, ghosts, bats, and donuts); pencils; glue; table salt; powdered tempera paint; and Q-tips.

Have the children trace symbols close together on a piece of construction paper, then cover some of the shapes with a thin coat of glue. Sprinkle colored salt, made by mixing salt and powdered tempera, over the glue. When the glue dries, shake off the excess salt. Repeat the process using different colors.

Or, have children cut the symbols from bright colored construction paper and glue them close together on the black paper.

Prayer Service—Fear Not, For He Is With Us

Opening Song: "Be Not Afraid" by Bob Dufford, S.J. (NALR), or "His Banner Over Me Is Love" by Carey Landry (NALR), or another suitable song.

Leader   Loving God, you sent your son to teach us of your love and to be with us always. Help us to remember this when we are nervous or afraid. We ask this through Christ our Lord.

All   Amen.

Reader 1   The Lord be with you.

All   And also with you.

Reader 1   A reading from the holy Gospel according to Matthew (28:16–20)

All   Glory to you, Lord.

Reader 1   (after the reading) The Gospel of the Lord.

All   Praise to you, Lord Jesus Christ.

Leader   In this Gospel, Jesus tells us that he will always be with us. He is with us in good times and bad. He is with us today as we gather in his name, and he is with us when we are alone and afraid.

What are some of the things you are afraid of? (Answers will vary, but will probably include fear of the dark.) We've probably all been afraid of the dark at one time or another, but remember that Jesus came to be our comfort and strength. He knows that darkness can be scary, so he described himself as the "Light of the World." Jesus will light up the dark times in our lives. We never have to be afraid of anything. We will have peace in our hearts if we learn to "turn over" our worries and problems to him. Sometimes we have to do this over and over until we truly learn to leave our problems with Jesus and not worry about them again.

Now let us pray together that we will remember that Jesus is always with us. Our response is: Jesus is with us.

Reader 2 When we're afraid of the dark, we pray . . .

All Jesus is with us.

Reader 3 When we're feeling alone, we pray . . .

All Jesus is with us.

Reader 4 When someone we love is sick, we pray . . .

All Jesus is with us.

Reader 5 When our parents get mad at us or don't understand us, we pray . . .

All Jesus is with us.

Reader 6 When we see violence and war on the news, we pray . . .

All Jesus is with us.

Reader 7 When we have problems with our friends, we pray . . .

All Jesus is with us.

Leader Loving God, you sent your son, Jesus, to be with us. Help us to know he is at our side when we are troubled. Help us to remember the great love that you have for each of us and to trust that you will help us, no matter what happens in our lives. We ask this in the name of Jesus, our Lord and brother.

All Amen.

Taking the Message Home

"Treating" the Poor

It's very exciting to go out "trick-or-treating"—in effect, begging for candy. Sadly, for many children throughout the world—even here in the United States—begging is not a game but a daily reality. They must beg from strangers or they will not eat.

As you enjoy this fun-filled "begging holiday," think of ways you can help those less fortunate than you are. Color in the pumpkin each time you do something to help the poor. Add new ideas as you think of them.

Pray that you'll find ways to help the poor.

Clean your closet and give your good, unused clothes to _____.

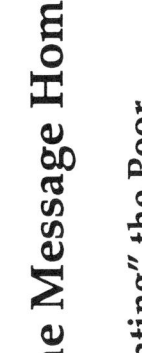

Clean your drawers and give the good things to _____.

Give away some Halloween candy to _____.

Earn money by _____ and give to UNICEF, Holy Childhood, or _____.

Eat a simple meal and give the money you saved to _____.

Reprinted with permission from *Celebrating Holidays* by Stacy Schumacher and Jim Fanning
1994 Twenty-Third Publications, P.O. Box 180, Mystic, CT 06355. 800-321-0411

5

Thanksgiving
A Time for Gratitude

Thanksgiving is a holiday with distinctly religious overtones, but catechists cannot assume that children are tuned into its religious meaning—no matter how well celebrated it is by our secular society. Pilgrims, Indians, and turkeys are important to our traditional celebrations, but they can distract from the real meaning of the feast. As a rule, our children have much to be grateful for, but they do not realize how greatly blessed they are. Reminding them not to take their blessings for granted can help them get into the true spirit of Thanksgiving.

Paulo's Busy Day

Paulo opened his eyes and saw the bright, early morning sun streaming in the window. He got up from his thin mat, careful not to wake his brothers and sisters on the mats around him. They would be going to school later and they needed their sleep. Some days Paulo joined them in the crowded schoolroom, but not today. Today he had to earn money. Since he slept in the only clothes he had, it did not take him long to get ready for work.

Silently, Paulo stepped out into the street. People were coming out of their small houses—some made of metal, some of plywood, and some only of cardboard—to head for work. Paulo hurried through the busy streets. Even this early, he could tell it was going to be hot. He waved to some friends, already playing in the alley.

Paulo hurried on, carrying his shoeshine kit on his back. He wanted to leave the barrio and get to the part of town where the rich people lived. There he would shine shoes and earn money for his family.

His mother worked hard every day, washing the clothes of the rich people. She wasn't paid much, so Paulo helped bring in money two or three days a week. He knew his mother sometimes lost hope, so he did what he could to keep her spirits high.

Paulo remembered what his friend Fernando had read from the Bible on Wednesday night. Fernando was a leader of their small community of faith. He had read them the story of the wedding banquet from the Gospel of Matthew. "Jesus told this story to give us hope," Fernando had explained. "We know we are among those invited to the great feast. We who are called in from the highways and byways support each other and keep alive esperanza."

Paulo liked meeting with this group on Wednesdays, but he was glad today was Friday. Tomorrow would be another full day of work, but then it would be Sunday, a day of rest, a day to go to church with his family. Word was that Father José was even going to be there to celebrate Mass this week! Paulo was happy and thankful at the thought of receiving communion.

He smiled as he saw himself reflected in the shoes that he had just shined. The man wearing them smiled too, and gave Paulo some money. "Thank you," said the man. "Thank you," said Paulo. He had already shined five pairs of shoes today, and all before noon! Some days it took 12 hours to get this much business. "Yes," Paulo thought, "I have much to be thankful for."

Talking It Over

1. Compare your life with Paulo's. What are the differences? In what ways is your life the same?

2. List the things Paulo is thankful for. Are you surprised that he is hopeful? Why? Why not?

Activity— Thanksgiving Word Search
Have the children do the puzzle on page 29.

Prayer Service—Thanksgiving
Opening Song: "Thank You, Lord," by Diane Davis (From *Hi God!* album), or another suitable song.

Leader	Heavenly Father, you have given us many gifts. Help us to be thankful for all we have and to show our gratitude by sharing with those who have less than we do. We make this prayer in the name of Jesus, your son.
All	Amen.
Reader 1	A reading from the holy Gospel according to Luke (12:48, adapted) One day Jesus said to his followers, "Much will be required of the person to whom much has been given, and even more will be demanded of the person to whom even more has been given." The Gospel of the Lord.
All	Praise to you, Lord Jesus Christ.
Leader	*(pause to allow for silent reflection after each question)* •What do you think Jesus means by this saying? •Are there some things you have that you forget to say thanks for? •What about your home or apartment? What about electricity and indoor plumbing? •What about your TV, or your Walkman, or your computer? (Here in the United States children have so much. Many children in other parts of the world don't have these things, and some children may not even know such things exist.) •Is there one particular thing you can do today to show your gratitude for all that you have? •Is there one particular way you can share something you have with someone? (If it seems appropriate, pause here and invite the children to discuss as a group how they might share what they have.)
Leader	Let us now express our thanks to God in prayer (Psalm 65, adapted): Lord, to you we shout with joy!
All	Lord, to you we shout with joy!
Reader 2	O God, it is right for us to praise you. We are filled with the good things and the blessings you have given us.
All	Lord, to you we shout with joy!

Activity—Thanksgiving Word Search

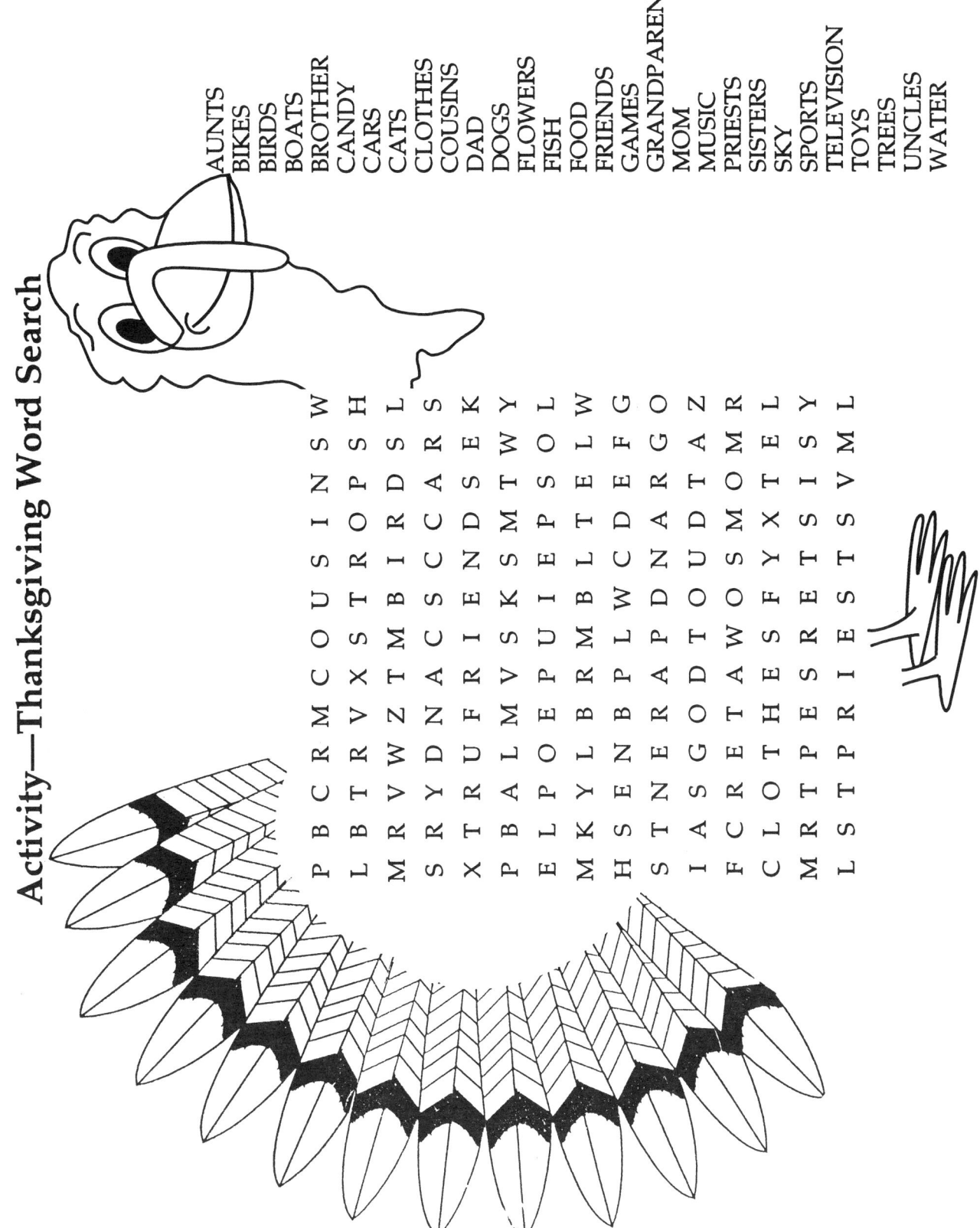

AUNTS
BIKES
BIRDS
BOATS
BROTHER
CANDY
CARS
CATS
CLOTHES
COUSINS
DAD
DOGS
FLOWERS
FISH
FOOD
FRIENDS
GAMES
GRANDPARENTS
MOM
MUSIC
PRIESTS
SISTERS
SKY
SPORTS
TELEVISION
TOYS
TREES
UNCLES
WATER

```
P B C R M C O U S I N S W
L B T R V X S T R O P S H
M R V W Z T M B I R D S L
S R Y D N A C S C C A R S
X T R U F R I E N D S E K
P B A L M V S K S M T W Y
E L P O E P U I E P S O L
M K Y L B R M B L T E L W
H S E N B P L W C D E F G
S T N E R A P D N A R G O
I A S G O D T O U D T A Z
F C R E T A W O S M O M R
C L O T H E S F Y X T E L
M R T P E S R E T S I S Y
L S T P R I E S T S V M L
```

Reprinted with permission from *Celebrating Holidays* by Stacy Schumacher and Jim Fanning
1994 Twenty-Third Publications, P.O. Box 180, Mystic, CT 06355. 800-321-0411

Reader 3	You have done amazing things for us, and people all over the world and across the oceans give you thanks. By your great power, you have made the mountains and calmed the roar of the ocean waves.
All	Lord, to you we shout with joy!
Reader 4	You show your care by sending rain to make the fields rich and fertile. You fill streams with water and provide crops on the land. What a rich harvest your goodness provides!
All	Lord, to you we shout with joy!

Litany of Thanks and Petition

Leader	You have given us many gifts, Lord. Teach us to share.
All	Lord, hear our prayer.
Leader	Our world is wonderful, overflowing with good things, Lord. Help us to care for it properly.
All	Lord, hear our prayer.
Leader	We have clothes to keep us warm and fashionable, Lord. Help us to share our excess with those in need.
All	Lord, hear our prayer.
Leader	For what else shall we pray, Lord? (Invite children to offer spontaneous prayers of thanks or petition.)
Leader	Please repeat after me: Loving Father, help us to appreciate all you have given us and to use well the gifts of life, freedom, nature, and the love you have given us. Forgive us for the times we are not thankful for all we have. Help us to remember those who are less fortunate, and to share with them what we can. We make this prayer in the name of Jesus, our savior and our brother. Amen.

Taking the Message Home

It Is Right to Give God Thanks

Write something for which you are grateful on each line below. Use the letter in the prayer as the beginning of each item you are thankful for. For example, for W you could thank God for wagons, windmills, water, or wisdom, or . . .

W_____

E _____

T _____

H_____

A _____

N_____

K_____

Y_____

O _____

U_____

L _____

O_____

R_____

D_____

Reprinted with permission from *Celebrating Holidays* by Stacy Schumacher and Jim Fanning 1994 Twenty-Third Publications, P.O. Box 180, Mystic, CT 06355. 800-321-0411

6

St. Nicholas Day

A Christmas Saint

Santa Claus, the hero of secular Christmas, is derived from a Christian saint. We can use the real Santa, Saint Nicholas, to bring children closer to the true meaning of the Christmas season. Their excitement about the jolly gift-giver can heighten their interest in his background—and the myths surrounding him can help us reclaim this season as a time to give generously and with joy.

It Is Better to Give

Sharlene looked at the calendar, her eye sparkling with excitement as she counted. "Nineteen days," she said. "Only nineteen days 'til Christmas!"

Her twin brother, Steve, brushed walnut shells from the table, "Only? Nineteen days is forever! Christmas will never get here!"

"Come on, Steve," said Uncle Doug as he brought more walnuts to the dining room table. "Waiting is half the fun!"

"I don't think so," frowned Steve. " It's too early to do anything real Christmasy, like putting up the tree or baking cookies."

"We're getting the fruitcake ingredients ready for Mom," offered Sharlene helpfully.

"I hate fruitcake," grumbled Steve.

"Okay, so you're having trouble waiting for Christmas," said Uncle Doug, "but what about today? This is a very important and exciting day."

"December 6 is important?"

"Yes! Saint Nicholas is important enough to have his feast day on the church calendar, and that day is today!"

"But who is he, Uncle Doug?" asked Sharlene. She felt sure her uncle would know because he was a teacher at their parish and he often taught them things about their faith.

"A long time ago," began Uncle Doug, "in the fourth century, Nicholas was a bishop in a place called Myra in Asia Minor. We call it Turkey now."

"We have a big turkey dinner on Christmas," said Steve. "Is that what St. Nicholas has to do with Christmas?"

"Very funny," grinned Uncle Doug, snatching the nutcracker away from his nephew. "Nicholas didn't start out as bishop, of course. His parents died when he was very young, and they left him a lot of money. For the rest of his life, Nicholas followed Jesus' example and gave to those in need. But the exciting thing about him is that no one ever caught him giving anything away." Uncle Doug's voice dropped to a whisper. "He did all his giving in secret!

"How?" asked Sharlene.

"We're not sure. In fact, there's a lot we don't know about Nicholas, because he kept all his good deeds a secret. But the most famous story about him says that he dropped bags of gold down the chimney of a house where three poor women lived. Without that money, the women couldn't have been married."

"A chimney?" asked Steve with new interest. "That sounds like Santa Claus."

"One of the bags of gold even landed in a stocking that had been hung by the fireplace to dry."

"That really sounds like Santa Claus!" said the twins together.

"Over the years the people of Holland developed a special devotion to Saint Nicholas," Uncle Doug continued. "And they celebrated December in a very special way. On the eve of Saint Nicholas's feast, they left their shoes outside the door—and in the morning they were filled with special gifts of candy and toys!"

"So Saint Nicholas invented the idea of the Christmas present?" asked Sharlene.

"I thought that was the three wise guys," said Steve.

"Wise men," laughed Uncle Doug. "But Nicholas certainly took the idea and ran with it, didn't he? Anyhow, when Dutch people began to settle in the New World, they brought their Christmas customs with them, including Nicholas, whom they called Sinter Klaas."

"That really sounds like Santa Claus!" exclaimed Steve. "Do you mean that Santa is really Saint Nicholas?"

"Well, it might help to think about that famous poem we read every Christmas."

"You mean 'Twas the Night Before Christmas?'" asked Sharlene, who could recite it from memory.

"That's what we usually call it," answered Uncle Doug, "but the author, Clement C. Moore, called it 'A Visit From Saint Nicholas.' The name Santa Claus is never mentioned."

"Wow!" said Steve. "Saint Nicholas sure is an important part of Christmas!"

"His example of giving just for the joy of it is one we can follow," smiled Uncle Doug. "In fact, why don't we make a list of what we're going to give others this Christmas?"

"We can leave them in our shoes tonight," suggested Sharlene excitedly, "so Santa, I mean, Saint Nicholas will be sure to see them."

"Sounds good to me," said Uncle Doug, throwing the last of the cracked walnuts into the big bowl. "What do you think, Steve?"

"I think Saint Nicholas shows that giving is what Christmas is all about. . . . And I'll make out a gift list if you make me a promise."

"What promise is that?"

Steve sighed and smiled at the same time. "Promise I won't have to eat any fruitcake!"

Talking It Over

1. Why do you think Santa Claus has become such an important part of our Christmas celebration? What does he have to do with the real meaning of Christmas?

2. Can you think of any stories from the Bible in which Jesus gives someone something? What does he give? What does he ask in return? What do you think that says to us?

3. Have you ever given something to someone and gotten something in return? Is it important to "receive" when we give? What do you think we get when we give way our love?

Activity—Saint Nicholas Door Hanger

A Saint Nicholas decoration, using a picture of Santa Claus, will help children connect our modern "symbol of greed" to the earlier sign of generosity.

Materials needed for each child: a 4" x 12" piece of construction paper (or light cardboard); a picture of Santa (from old cards, wrapping paper, magazines); and markers, scissors, and glue. Give children these instructions: Cutting in from one side, make a 1" circle in the middle of the paper about 1" from the top, and then glue the picture of Santa Claus in the center of the page. Write a prayer to Saint Nicholas around the picture (with markers). For example: "Saint Nicholas, help us give gifts with joy."

Prayer Service—Giving Is a Blessing

Opening Song: "The Whole World Is Waiting for Love" ("The Advent Song") by Sr. Marianne Misetich, or another appropriate song.

Leader	We're on our Advent journey to Christmas Day, but it seems like a very long trip sometimes! We can make good use of this time by considering the example of Saint Nicholas.
Reader 1	Many are the tales about Saint Nicholas and his generous giving.
Reader 2	The most famous story of the kind Bishop of Myra is how he helped a very poor man with a big problem.
Reader 3	"Dear Lord," the poor man prayed, "I have three daughters, but no money. Without money, no one will marry them—and if they are not married, they will have to be sold into slavery."
Reader 4	The poor man prayed for a miracle, because he knew only a miracle could give him what he needed.
Reader 1	The Lord must have heard the man's prayer because Nicholas learned of his problem.
Reader 2	That very night Nicholas climbed up on the roof of the poor man's house and dropped a bag of gold down the crumbling chimney.
Reader 3	In the morning, the overjoyed man and his oldest daughter thanked God for the gold that had miraculously appeared.
Reader 4	And the miracle happened twice more; the other two daughters each discovered a bag of gold.
Reader 1	One bag had even landed right in the third daughter's stocking, which she had hung by the fireplace.

Reader 2   From this story we know that, like Nicholas, we help spread God's love whenever we give to those in need.

Reader 3   Nicholas teaches us that giving to others gives us joy, too.

Leader   As a bishop, Nicholas knew the Bible very well, and we can be sure that the following passage from the Acts of the Apostles was one of his favorites (Acts 20:35, adapted).

Reader 4   Paul said, "I have shown you in all things that by working hard we must help the weak, remembering the words that the Lord Jesus himself said: 'There is more happiness in giving than in receiving.'"

Leader   Can you remember the first time you were excited about giving a gift to someone? Think about what it was and who it was for. Tell the person next to you about that gift. (Allow a minute or two for sharing, and then pray the closing prayer.)

Lord Jesus, the time for celebrating your birth is getting closer. As we prepare, help us to remember the example of Saint Nicholas, who truly found more joy in giving than in receiving. We ask this in your name.

All   Amen.

Taking the Message Home

Secret Goodness

In the days ahead, see how often you can do something good without getting caught at it. Fill in a gift for each time you succeed in imitating Saint Nicholas in this way.

7

Christmas
A Season for Jesus

What is Christmas really about? Is it celebrating a birthday with gifts, dinners, and family gatherings? Or is it about living out Jesus' love in our homes and neighborhoods? Even devoted followers of the Star of Bethlehem are sometimes distracted by "Christmas chores." We need to continuously refocus the students' attention so that everything they do as they prepare to celebrate the Lord's birth draws them closer to him.

The Christmas Star

Amy ran up the stairs, burst through the front door, and yelled, "I got it! I got it! I got the lead in the Christmas play!"

"That's great," said her mother. "What part are you playing?"

"I'm the doubting villager," Amy replied. "All the other people at Bethlehem try to tell me about what happened—but I don't believe them."

"Sounds like a great part, Amy. I'm so proud of you! Now, Honey, come on into the kitchen and let me show you what I've left for dinner. I've got to go to work."

Amy got instructions for dinner, said good-by to her mother, and then sat at the kitchen table eating cookies.

"I sure wish Mom hadn't taken an extra Christmas job," she thought. "I miss having her around after school."

Later, Amy shared her exciting news with her sister Theresa, her brother Raul, and her father. All were very happy for her, but couldn't spend much time talking about it; they each had so many things to do. It was hard to tell which member of the family was the busiest!

Two hectic weeks later, Amy asked Theresa, "Will you help me rehearse my lines? I've been studying them like mad . . . and I think I've got them."

"Sorry, Amy, I'm off to work," Theresa said. "I asked for extra hours so I can save money for Christmas presents."

Amy found Raul and asked for his help. "Wish I could help, Honey, but I'm on my way out the door. I've got to get some more Christmas shopping done. I can't even believe how many Christmas gifts I still have to buy!"

The day of the Christmas pageant finally arrived! At dinner time, Amy said, "Where's Theresa? I want to ask her to drive me over to school early to be there at 6:30. Then she can save seats for the rest of you."

"She got called into work, Amy—and I did, too" Mom answered regretfully. "The other clerk in my department got sick and, at this time of year, they have to have the shop fully staffed. Theresa got called in when her firm got a large Christmas order. There's just nothing we can do about it, Sweetheart," Mom added, seeing the hurt on Amy's face. "We're terribly disappointed!"

"You're disappointed!" screamed Amy, "What about me? Nobody cares about me! I've been getting ready for this stupid play for weeks. I hardly had time for anything else, and now no one will be there to see me! Where's our family's Christmas spirit?" With that she burst into tears and ran from the room.

She didn't get far. At the doorway she bumped into a tall, sturdy body and was surrounded by strong, warm arms. Clasping her to his chest, her father told her, "Amy, Amy, slow down. Everyone in this family loves you and wants to see you in your big part. Mom and Theresa have asked me to videotape the play for them, because they don't want to miss it. Don't blame them; feel sorry for them."

As Amy sniffed and considered this, he added, "And what do you mean, 'No one will be there' to see you? Raul and I will be there—we're each someone!"

Soon Amy dried her tears, got ready for her big moment, and went with part of her family to the auditorium. The play was a rousing success—and Amy delivered all of her many lines convincingly.

On the way home they stopped for a hot fudge sundae and Raul and her father could hardly stop congratulating Amy on how well she did in her starring role.

Back in the car Raul commented, "Our family has been way too busy this Christmas season. Theresa and Mom with their extra hours of work, me with marathon shopping, and even Amy with her play. We haven't had any time to do anything together—and Christmas is almost here!"

"You've got a point there," his father answered. "Maybe after life settles down, we should have a family meeting and see if we can learn from this hectic season—and schedule each other into next Christmas's preparation."

"Next year's too late," Amy put in, "Christmas is really about Jesus—and except for our Advent wreath, we haven't done much extra for him this season."

"I know!" Raul exclaimed, "School's out now, so maybe tomorrow you and I can bake some cookies and take them to a nursing home!"

"Good idea, Raul!" Dad replied. "It's a good start, and we have a little time to work on real preparation a bit more before Christmas is actually here. How about singing Christmas carols until we get home?"

"That's more like real Christmas spirit," smiled Amy. "We'll show we know who the real star of Christmas is!"

Talking It Over

1. If a non-Christian person saw your family's Christmas preparations, could she tell what, or who, was being celebrated?

2. What are some of the ways your family brings Jesus into Christmas planning and preparing?

3. Think of some new ways your family could spread Jesus' love during the Christmas season.

Activity—Star Ornament

Materials needed: school picture or other small portrait; yellow, gold, or white felt; gold embroidery thread; embroidery needles; glue; glitter or sequins.

Cut a star—or two or three graduated ones—out of white, yellow, or gold felt. Glue the student's picture in the center, with one point over the head. Add decorations to the points, gluing sequins around the picture and down the points. Thread the needle and make a loop at the end of the top point for a hanger.

Tell the children to remember as they add this ornament to their tree that they are reflections of the light of the true Christmas Star.

Prayer Service—The Lord Is with Us

Opening Song: "O Come, All Ye Faithful," or another Christmas carol.

Leader	We come together to thank our loving God for the gift of Jesus and for the chance to celebrate his birth into our world. Please repeat this prayer after me: God of Love, your son, Jesus, is your greatest gift to us. He is a sign of your love, a love so immense we cannot imagine it. Help us always to walk in your love and to put you and Jesus first in our lives. We pray in the name of Jesus, our brother and our Lord. Amen.
Reading	A reading from the holy Gospel according to Luke (2:8–16) (This reading can easily be acted out with or without simple costumes and props.)
Reader 1	There were shepherds in the hills, keeping watch over their sheep throughout the night. Suddenly an angel of the Lord appeared to them, with the glory of the Lord shining around them. The shepherds fell to the ground afraid.
Angel 1	Don't be afraid. I have come to bring you good news, news of joy for all people. Today a savior has been born to you in the town of David. He is the Messiah and the Lord. Let this be a sign for you: You will find a baby wrapped in swaddling clothes and lying in a manger.
Reader 1	Just then the angel was surrounded by many more angels. They all gave praise to God.
Angels	Glory to God in the highest. Peace to all on Earth, for God is blessing the people.
Reader 2	When the angels had left them and gone back to heaven, the shepherds talked among themselves about what they should do.

Shepherd	Let us go to Bethlehem and see what the Lord has told us about.
Reader 2	So they came in a great hurry and there they found Mary and Joseph with the baby wrapped in swaddling clothes and lying in the manger. The Gospel of the Lord.
All	Praise to you, Lord Jesus Christ.

Reflection	The shepherds dropped everything to go see Jesus. They even left their sheep out in the fields. Once they heard the Good News, they just had to respond.
	    It might be easier for us to respond completely if we heard a choir of angels telling us the news. But we don't! What are some of the ways we hear the Good News today? We're not called to drop everything and go looking for Jesus. What are some of the ways we're asked to respond?
	    Jesus has come and is with us. We don't get a signal telling us to look for him in swaddling clothes in a manger. Instead, he's here in many ways. One of the hardest things for us to do is to learn to find Jesus in our everyday lives. What are some of the ways he is with us today? As we close our prayer service, let's pray that Jesus will come more deeply into our lives and that we will clearly see him with us. Our response is: Come, Lord Jesus.

Reader 3	Into our lives, we pray . . .
All	Come, Lord Jesus.
Reader 3	Into our homes, we pray . . .
All	Come, Lord Jesus.
Reader 3	Into our baking, shopping, and wrapping, we pray . . .
All	Come, Lord Jesus.
Reader 3	Into our gift giving, we pray . . .
All	Come, Lord Jesus.
Reader 3	Into our troubled world, we pray . . .
All	Come, Lord Jesus.
Reader 3	Into the poor and the needy, we pray . . .

All	Come, Lord Jesus.
Reader 3	Into our Christmas joy, we pray . . .
All	Come, Lord Jesus.
Leader	Lord Jesus, help us to see you, to follow you, and to bring your love to others as we celebrate the day of your birth with enthusiastic joy. Amen.
	Closing Song: "Joy to the World."

Taking the Message Home

Share Christmas Love

Make a list of all the people you know who might be lonely or unhappy this Christmas season. Consider your relatives, neighbors, people you pray for at church. List them below:

_____   _____
_____   _____
_____   _____
_____   _____
_____   _____
_____   _____
_____   _____
_____   _____
_____   _____
_____   _____
_____   _____
_____   _____
_____   _____

Think of ways that you could spread Christmas cheer to these people. One of your parents might be able to help you. Some ideas are: Send a Christmas card or letter, go to visit, make cookies or another Christmas goody to take to some of those on your list, offer to help someone with yard or housework. Each time you spread Christmas cheer, give yourself a star—or a Christmas sticker. Enjoy bringing *joy* to your part of the *world*!

Reprinted with permission from *Celebrating Holidays* by Stacy Schumacher and Jim Fanning 1994 Twenty-Third Publications, P.O. Box 180, Mystic, CT 06355. 800-321-0411

New Year's Day
A New Beginning

As Catholics, we commemorate January 1 as a holy day, the Solemnity of Mary, Mother of God, but we also celebrate it as New Year's Day with the rest of our nation. We can help our students make a spiritual connection when they ring in the New Year by exploring the idea of resolutions, those special promises we make at the start of a new year to help us change. We are always trying to change, to become more and more converted to God's way of looking at the life God has given us.

Off to a Good Start

Robert woke up early on New Year's Day. He quietly went down to the kitchen, made a pitcher of orange juice, and sipped juice while he set the table for breakfast. Uncertain what to do next, he referred to a sheet propped up on the counter: "New Year's Resolutions," his list of five ways he was going to try to be a better person in the year ahead:

1. Don't always get angry.
2. Help around the house without being asked.
3. Take the dog for a walk every day.
4. Don't fight with Peter.
5. Remember to pray first thing in the morning.

"Uh oh," Robert thought, "I didn't pray! I've already broken one of my resolutions and the year is only eight hours old!" Quickly he said a silent prayer. Besides offering his day to the Lord, Robert asked Jesus to help him keep his New Year's resolutions.

"I could take the dog for a walk," he thought, "but first I think I'll check out the Rose Parade." Turning on the TV, Robert congratulated himself for starting the day by helping to get breakfast ready and by setting the table. "If only I had remembered to pray," he thought, "my New Year would be off to a perfect start."

Peter, Robert's younger brother, came into the room and instantly started complaining about the parade. Peter wanted to watch the early morning cartoons.

"The cartoons aren't on this morning," Robert patiently explained. "It's New Year's Day and parades are on instead. Tomorrow you can see cartoons. Do you want some orange juice?"

"I want soda!" Peter screamed. "And I don't want to watch this stupid parade, I want my cartoons!"

"You can't have soda for breakfast, Peter," Robert said. "Now quiet down! You're going to wake Mom and she wants to sleep late this morning!"

Turning back to the television, Robert noticed that one of the most spectacular floats was coming down the street. It was a gigantic clown juggling small clowns. "Are they mechanical," Robert wondered, "or could they be real people?" As he peered closely at the screen, it suddenly went black. Peter, holding the remote, said, "I want cartoons!"

This was too much for Robert! He grabbed the remote, and gave Peter a whack on the back.

"Mom," screamed the annoying child, "Robert pounded me for no reason!"

Mom appeared on the steps. "Robert," she said, "why can't you try to get along with Peter? You're 12 years old. You'd think you could act more grown up than your four-year-old brother!"

"I'm sorry, Mom," responded Robert, "but he was being a real brat."

"Robert, as the oldest, you're supposed to set a good example," his mother said. "And you are never to hit your brother! Go to your room. You can come down when breakfast is ready."

Grabbing his list, Robert stomped up the stairs, thinking how unfair his mother always was. "Not even 9:00, and I've already broken most of my resolutions," he groaned. "It's no use. I never do anything right. I might as well give up." He threw himself on the bed.

Ten minutes later his mother found him there. "I'm sorry I yelled at you, Robert. I know how annoying Peter can be. He's going through a terrible stage right now, but he will outgrow it, and we have to try to be patient with him."

"I know," replied Robert, "but I get so mad at him and I can't change—no matter how hard I try!"

Explaining to his mother about his broken resolutions, Robert told her how useless it was to expect him to ever be any better.

"Change is hard, Robert, and it takes time," his mother pointed out. "You can't expect to change everything you don't like about yourself all at once. You've made a good start just by making that list of what you want to change."

"What good does that do, if I still keep doing them?"

"Once you decide to change," his mother answered, "the next thing is to become aware of your actions. Becoming aware is an important step in changing. Once you start recognizing what you want to fix, you are a lot closer to really changing it. . . And remember, it's almost impossible to change lots of things all at once. It's much better to try to work on one or two things at a time. Then when you're on your way with those, you can add something else. Let's look at your list and see what you might start with."

They both agreed that getting along with Peter was the most important thing for him to work on.

"Try not to hit Peter," his mother suggested, "and apologize as quickly as you can if you do smack him. Soon you'll get in the habit of telling him that you're annoyed, instead of hitting or yelling at him."

"Then I can go to work on something else on my list!" Robert said.

"Right!" his mother added, "and by the way, Honey, thanks a lot for fixing the juice and setting the table."

Talking It Over

1. Have you ever made a resolution? Was it as difficult for you to keep as it was for Robert to keep his? Why or why not?

2. Why do people make resolutions at New Year's? What are some other good times to make resolutions?

3. We know that God loves us just as we are—so why should we try to change ourselves with resolutions?

Activity—A New Year's Noisemaker
People often ring in the New Year with noisemakers. The children can make some colorful shakers to remind them of the excitement of starting over in the New Year.

Materials needed: toilet paper tubes; 4 1/2" x 4 1/2" pieces of colorful wrapping paper; 2 small scraps of paper, for each tube's ends; handful of beans, rice, or unpopped popcorn; strips of tissue paper, about 4 1/2" x 8"; white glue; masking tape.

Have the children cover one end of the tube with a piece of scratch paper, taping it with two crossing strips of masking tape. Then they pour in a handful of beans, rice, or popcorn and close up the other end of the tube. Let them choose a piece of wrapping paper and wrap it around the tube and glue it in place. Holding the short side of the tissue paper, they cut a fringe in it, cutting to within 1" of the edge. (Prepare this ahead of time for young children.) Apply glue liberally to one end of the wrapped tube and wrap the tissue paper around it. Wait awhile for the glue to dry—overnight, if possible. Then shake and make a joyful noise to the Lord!

Prayer Service—Lord, Help Us to Change
(Note: Have a pencil and a small sheet of paper ready for each child.)
Opening Song: "Hi God!" by Carey Landry, or any lively song that the class knows. (Invite the children to shake their noisemakers as they sing.)

Leader   Repeat after me:

Creator God,
thank you for the gift
of this New Year.
Help us to find you
in every day, every hour, every minute
of the year ahead of us. Amen.

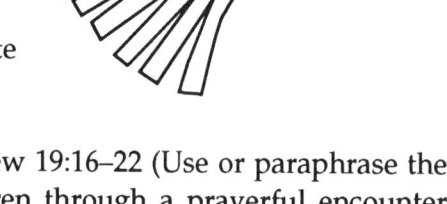

Guided Meditation based on Matthew 19:16–22 (Use or paraphrase the following words to guide the children through a prayerful encounter with Jesus.)

Boys and girls, today we are going to pray in a special way, but first we need to get ready. (If this form of praying is new to your students, tell them that they may feel a bit awkward, but they need to be very quiet so they can think about what you are saying and not disturb others.)

Sit up straight, rest your hands in your lap, and close your eyes. Think about your breathing, trying to make it slow and even—as you breathe in deeply . . . and breathe out . . . Breathe in God's love, breathe out bad feelings . . . With your eyes still closed, picture yourself in a grassy field on a beautiful, sunny day. Feel the soft breeze on your face as you look around. You see other children and men and women, too. You can tell from their long robes and sandals that you are back in Bible times . . . As you look around, you see that all these people are listening to a man sitting under a tree . . . Looking closer, you see that it is Jesus. You walk through the crowd, coming nearer to Jesus, trying to hear what he is saying . . .

Suddenly, you see a young man walking up to Jesus. From his colorful, silken robes and the gold rings on his fingers you can tell that he is rich . . . You hear him ask Jesus, "What good must I do to receive eternal life?"

Jesus replies, "If you want to be perfect, go and sell all you have and give the money to the poor. Then come follow me." . . . The young man's smile fades away into a frown, and you see him walk sadly away. Jesus looks at the crowd . . . Then he looks at you . . . Jesus comes over to you, puts his hand on your shoulder, and lovingly looks into your face . . . "What about you?" he asks. "What do you have trouble letting go of, so you can follow me? The rich young man wouldn't even try to think about it. Will you? . . . What is there in your life that needs changing? What part of your life will you try to live better this new year?" Tell Jesus about it . . .

Now you hear Jesus tell you he will help you change in the year ahead. He tells you how much he loves you. He gives you a big hug . . . You have to get back, so you leave Jesus in the field. You're returning to our classroom now . . . Your breathing is calm and peaceful, and slowly you open your eyes.

Share with one person how you felt during this prayer. Were you comfortable? Could you speak with Jesus? Did it seem that he was with you? (We are all different and won't react the same to this kind of prayer, but for some it is a wonderful way to get in touch with the Lord.)

Writing Your Resolution
Ask the children to think some more about what they want to change in the new year. Maybe one will decide to help more around the house, another to be nice to a brother or sister, still another to try to be nice to a classmate who needs a friend. Whatever they decide to do is their resolution—a special promise to try to keep. (Hand out small pieces of paper.) Tell the students, "Now write out your resolution, and remember as you do so that Jesus is always with you to help you try to become a more loving person." When the children have finished writing, collect the resolutions. Give them back periodically throughout the year and invite the children to discuss how they are doing in keeping their resolutions.

Closing Song: "New Hope" or "Signs of New Life" by Carey Landry, or any song that the students know and enjoy. One again, have them shake the noisemakers while they sing.

Taking the Message Home

Remembering Your Resolution

Put a check mark (✔) for each time you *think* of your resolution and a happy face for each time you *keep* it.

Day 1 _____

Day 2 _____

Day 3 _____

Day 4 _____

Day 5 _____

Day 6 _____

Day 7 _____

Day 8 _____

Day 9 _____

Day 10 _____

Day 11 _____

Day 12 _____

Day 13 _____

Day 14 _____

Don't give up! Sometimes it takes quite a while to change!
(Hang this on your mirror or on the refrigerator—where you'll see it often.)

Reprinted with permission from *Celebrating Holidays* by Stacy Schumacher and Jim Fanning 1994 Twenty-Third Publications, P.O. Box 180, Mystic, CT 06355. 800-321-0411

9
Martin Luther King Day
Dreaming of a Better World

Martin Luther King's Birthday is a real cause for celebration! This unique holiday honors a great civil rights leader who lived fully the difficult Gospel call to "love your enemies." It challenges students (and adults) of every ethnic background to follow Dr. King's example and to believe that one person can make a real difference. Help your children more deeply appreciate the importance of perseverance in working toward the fulfillment of their dreams as you celebrate this holiday.

Vicki's Video

Anne leaned back and considered her drawing of Martin Luther King. Her class was working on projects to honor Dr. King, whose birthday would be celebrated at an assembly in school the following week.

As Anne reached for another blue crayon to color in the sky on her drawing, she sensed someone looking over her shoulder. Turning quickly, Anne was startled to see a video camera staring down at her.

"Oh, Vicki!" breathed Anne, as her classmate peered out from behind the camera. "You scared me!"

"Sorry," said Vicki. "I'm getting ready for my 'Kid on the Street' interviews next week."

"You're not really going to do that, are you?" asked Anne in an exasperated tone.

"I've always wanted to make a video," said Vicki, giving her father's camera a pat as she set it down, "and Mrs. Henderson said I could."

"A video will be so hard, Vicki," said Anne. "Why don't you just draw a picture or make a poster like everyone else?"

"This is what I want to do," replied Vicki, a little surprised at Anne's attitude. "Besides, I'll have help. Walter and Billy said they wanted to do some taping."

"Big help they'll be," muttered Anne, turning back to her coloring. "All they want to do is fool around with your camera."

Vicki felt discouraged. She was counting on her friends for help, or at least support. She knew that her video project was too difficult to do on her own. But as she looked around the classroom and saw everyone hard at work on their art projects, Vicki recalled the many things Mrs. Henderson and the class had discovered about Dr. King.

It took real courage for Martin Luther King to be nonviolent when others were violent toward him. Many people thought he was wrong; even people he tried to help called him "Martin Loser King" because he believed in returning love for hatred.

"But he never gave up," thought Vicki. "He always worked to make his dream a reality. And Dr. King didn't rely on others to fight for him. He did what he believed in, no matter what anyone else did."

Vicki picked up her camera. There would be a lot of activities next week and everyone would be thinking about Martin Luther King. Vicki resolved that she would tape as many of these as she could.

Two weeks later, right after lunch, Mrs. Henderson surprised her class by wheeling a TV and VCR to the middle of the room. "Even though we celebrated Martin Luther King's birthday last week," she said, turning on the TV, "we're never finished celebrating his dream. To help us keep that in mind, we're going to see a dream come true."

"Is this a video about Dr. King?" asked Anne.

"Is it a cartoon?" called out Billy.

"It's Vicki's video," smiled Mrs. Henderson. "And as we watch her report on what our school did and what our students were thinking, we'll see that Martin Luther King wasn't the only one who could work to make a dream come true."

As Vicki's video flashed on the TV screen, Anne leaned over and whispered, "I thought you gave up."

"I almost did," said Vicki. "But then I remembered Martin Luther King. He had a dream that was a lot bigger and harder than mine, and he didn't give up. He was only one person but he went ahead and did everything he could to make that dream come true. And when he did, lots of people helped him—just like lots of people helped me—my mom and dad, Mrs. Henderson, even Walter and Billy."

"I didn't think you could do it," admitted Anne, "but now I really want to see your video!"

"Thanks," grinned Vicki as she too turned toward the TV.

Talking It Over

1. Have you ever had a dream? Did it come true? What did you have to do to make it come true?

2. Martin Luther King kept working toward his dream of equality, even when it seemed hopeless. Have you ever kept at a project when things looked difficult or impossible? How did you overcome the challenges?

3. Because of Dr. King's efforts, life improved for many people, yet discrimination and injustice still exist. What can *you* do to keep Martin Luther King's dream alive?

Activity—Discovering the Message

See the activity on page 54. One line from a famous civil rights song describes the basic belief that kept Dr. King going. Using the code, do the math and you'll uncover this inspiring verse.

Prayer Service—We All Have a Dream

Opening Song: "Only a Shadow" by Carey Landry, or any appropriate song familiar to your group.

Leader Why would God want us to love others as we love our own selves? *(Pause for responses.)* Yes, God made us all—and we are, each and every one of us, made in his image and likeness. So, even though we have differences, people all over the world have lots more similarities and variations. What are some ways you are just like children in China, Africa, and Europe? *(Pause for responses.)* You're right, all the things you mentioned are things we have in common—and we could go on all day listing other ways we're alike.

Probably the most important way they are like us is that we are all loved by the same God and have the power to love others. If we real-

___ ___ ___ ___   ___ ___   ___ ___
5+5 3+1 2+2 15+2 5+4 10+1 1+1 0+1

___ ___   ___   ___   ___   ___   ___ ___
5+3 10−6 2+4   11+1 6+1   8+1   7+3 3+2

___   ___ ___   ___ ___ ____ ___
3+10 0+4 1+15 8+1 5−1 10+4 8−4

"___   ___   ___   ____ ___   ____   ____
 10+5 6−2   2+1   10−2 9−3   10+6   13+3

___ ___ ____ ___ ____ ____ ___ ____
1+4 7+7 11−7 6+6 8+10 11−6 1+1 12−8

___ ____ ____ ___   ___ ___ ____."
6−3 10−5 10−8 0+4   3+7 5+1 10−9

1=Y, 2=M, 3=S, 4=E, 5=O, 6=A, 7=T, 8=H, 9=I, 10=D, 11=N, 12=R,

13=B, 14=V, 15=W, 16=L, 17=P, 18=C

ly lived the law that the lawyer recited to Jesus, what a wonderful world we would have! That's what Martin Luther King worked for and died for.

Reader 2 We'll now respond to God's Word using the words of Dr. King. Our response is: I have a dream.

Reader 1 I have a dream that one day little black boys and black girls will be able to join hands with little white boys and white girls as sisters and brothers.

All I have a dream.

Reader 2 I have a dream that my four little children one day will live in a nation where they will not be judged by the color of their skin but by the content of their character.

All I have a dream.

Reader 3 I have a dream that one day the glory of the Lord will be revealed and all flesh shall see it together.

All	I have a dream.
Reader 4	I have a dream of freedom ringing from every mountaintop, from every hilltop.
All	I have a dream.
Reader 5	And when we allow freedom to ring from every state and city, we will be able to speed up that day when all of God's children will be able to join hands and say . . .
Reader 6	"Free at last, free at last, thank God almighty, we are free at last."
All	I have a dream.
Leader	Generous God, thank you for making us dreamers. Help our dreams to come true so the world will be a better place for all your children. We pray in the name of Jesus.
All	Amen.

Taking the Message Home

Loving My Neighbor

Write down the names of some people you find difficult to love. Watch them in the days ahead. Put a ✔ when you see them doing a kind or generous thing. Make an **X** when you see him or her do something the way you might have done it. Draw an **O** as a sign that you have recognized a unique gift or talent in the person you're trying to love.

At the end of a week, circle the face that shows how you feel about that person now.

10

Valentine's Day
Love One Another

Greeting card companies and florists have made Valentine's Day into one of the major holidays of the year. The message of the day, however, is a vital one, whether from secular or church voices: Love others and show your loved ones that you love them. This holiday provides the religion teacher with an excellent opportunity to restate and celebrate this important truth—and to introduce an interesting Christian saint. Even though the details of Valentine's life are lost in the uncertainties of unrecorded history, still, the myths are fun—and can make some good points.

The Man with a Big Heart

Long, long ago, about three hundred years after Jesus' resurrection from the dead, Claudius II, the Roman emperor, wanted everyone to worship gods he thought were true. "These Christians say Jesus is God. They pray to him," he said. "I'll put a stop to that!" And he made it a crime to believe in Jesus.

A priest named Valentine lived in Rome at that time. He loved Jesus and told everyone he could about him—his life, death, and resurrection. "Please, Father Valentine," his friends begged, "stop talking about Jesus in public. It's against the law and is going to get you into big trouble."

"I can't do that," exclaimed Valentine. "Telling people about Jesus and his love is my life's work! The Good News can't be hidden from those who need to hear it."

In no time at all, the fears of Valentine's friends proved true and Valentine was arrested and thrown in jail.

His jailer saw how kind and wise the gentle priest was. "I probably shouldn't ask you a favor when you are in such trouble," the jailer said to Valentine, "but would you consider teaching my daughter Julia? She is bright and wants to learn about the world, but sadly she has been blind since birth."

"I would be happy to teach her!" Valentine replied, smiling at the burly man whose tender love for his daughter shone in his face. "Giving lessons will help me pass the time here in this prison. Bring her to me!"

So Valentine taught Julia. They each looked forward to the lessons. Julia was bright, as well as beautiful. She quickly learned much about math, history, and the world around her. Valentine became Julia's eyes, so naturally she saw things as he did. She soon knew all about Jesus and his love, and loved him in return! "Whenever we speak in love, the Lord hears us," said Valentine one day.

With her sightless eyes shining, Julia answered, "I have been speaking to him. Every day I pray that my eyes will be healed, as he healed the blind when he was on Earth. I would so like to see the world you have taught me about!"

Touched by the young girl's faith, Valentine replied, "Jesus told the blind man, 'If you believe, you will see.'"

"Oh, Father Valentine, I do believe, I surely do," Julia said.

The jail cell was dark and quiet as Julia and Valentine prayed together. Suddenly, "Father, what is all that brightness?" Julia cried. Valentine saw only the reflected starlight through the window, but realized immediately what Julia was seeing.

"God has given you your sight, Julia. You are seeing the light outside," Valentine said with a smile. Together the two of them praised God for this wonderful miracle.

Not long afterward, Valentine received word that his execution date was set. Even when facing his own death, he worried about others. He was concerned that Julia and her father might forget about Jesus and his love when he was not there to teach and remind them.

The night before he was to be executed, Valentine wrote a last note to Julia: "Today you can read this with your own eyes," he wrote on the scratchy parchment. "Never forget that you are a living sign of God's power and love. I look forward to seeing you once again in the heavenly kingdom." Then he stopped for a moment to think of how he'd end this final message. Smiling, he signed the letter, "From your Valentine."

The next day, February 14, Father Valentine was killed for refusing once again to worship the false gods of Rome. Each year on the date of his death we remember how he showed Jesus' love to others. We send our notes of love—and call them "Valentines."

Talking It Over

1. Valentine died for his faith. Have you ever had to stand up for your faith when people misunderstood you or made fun of you? How did it feel? How could the example of St. Valentine help you in a situation like that?

2. Read the Gospel story of the blind man's healing (Luke 18:35–43). How is the healing of Julia's sight similar?

3. St. Valentine brought the light of Christ into Julia's dark world, even before her healing. How might you do the same for others?

4. What are some reasons we consider Valentine to be a saint? Are you also called to be a saint? In what ways?

Activity—Valentine Bookmarks

Materials needed: red, white, and pink felt; glue; scissors; markers.

Cut a 8" strip of red felt for each child. Let each choose three 2" squares from which to fold and cut hearts. Then have them glue these down the red strip, writing "I" on the top one and "You" on the bottom heart. (If you have more time, and don't mind messy clean-up, let them glue glitter around the edges of the hearts. Children love glitter!)

Prayer Service—Loved, Lovable, and Loving

(Note: Children will need heart-shaped paper.)
Opening Song: "They'll Know We Are Christians," "What Makes Love Grow," by Carey Landry, or another suitable song.

Leader   God is our loving creator, who sent his son, Jesus, to teach us how to be loving brothers and sisters and so we pray: God of love, you gave us parents and friends to show us your love. Help us to bring your love to all we meet. Give us strength, O Lord, to be loving toward those who are hard to love or who are not kind to us. We ask this in the name of Jesus.

All   Amen.

Reader 1	A reading from the first letter of John (3:1,16–19) (after the reading) The Word of the Lord.
All	Thanks be to God.
Leader	Think for a few moments about how much love Jesus has for you. He came to Earth for you. He lived as a human being, feeling hunger, sorrow, and joy for you. He died and rose from the dead for you. Now close your eyes and sit up straight in your chairs. Breathe in slowly and deeply, breathe out all the air you have taken in . . . Breathe in Jesus' love . . . Breathe it out so that it surrounds you . . . Feel Jesus' love within and around you . . . Perhaps you experience it as a warm place inside, or a blanket around yourself, or a sense of his loving presence . . . Thank Jesus for his love . . . Ask him to help you show his love to others . . . Now slowly open your eyes. Try to remember the feeling of Jesus' love throughout the day.

Give each child a paper heart and ask them to write the names of people they love on it. Pass a basket and let everyone put their hearts in it. Ask a student to raise the basket as the leader prays:

Leader	Jesus, bless those whose names we have written. Give them all that they need and as much of what they want as is good for them. When they need you most, help them to feel your presence.
All	Amen.
Reader 1	As we pray together, please respond: Lord, help us to love.
Reader 2	For our parents, grandparents, teachers, sisters and brothers, and all who love and care for us, we pray . . .
All	Lord, help us to love.
Reader 3	For our friends and classmates, we pray . . .
All	Lord, help us to love.
Reader 4	For those who don't feel loved, we pray . . .
All	Lord, help us to love.
Reader 1	For those who are difficult for us to love, we pray . . .
All	Lord, help us to love.

Reader 2	For the poor who need our loving help, we pray . . .
All	Lord, help us to love.
Reader 3	For the world, which is in great need of love, we pray . . .
All	Lord, help us to love.
Reader 4	For all our special Valentines, we pray . . .
All	Lord, help us to love.
Leader	Loving God, you call us all to be your sons and daughters and to reflect your love to others. May your love glow within us and shine on everyone we see. We pray in Jesus' name.
All	Amen.
Leader	As a sign of our relationship to God and one another, let us join hands and pray together the prayer that Jesus taught us. Our Father…

Taking the Message Home

Loving the Unlovable

Almost everyone has some people who are hard to love, who annoy you or make you uncomfortable. Sometimes it can be a brother or sister who gets on your nerves. Pick one of these people and spend a week being extra kind to this person. Some suggestions:

- Pray for her or him each day—perhaps several times a day.
- Try to notice something good about the person.
- Compliment him or her when possible. (Be sure your compliments are sincere.)
- Send the person a friendly Valentine, note, or little gift.

Give yourself a heart every time you remember to do some good toward your difficult person.

Day 1 _____ ♥

Day 2 _____ ♥

Day 3 _____ ♥

Day 4 _____ ♥

Day 5 _____ ♥

Day 6 _____ ♥

Day 7 _____ ♥

At the end of the week, write a sentence or two about how you now feel about the person. If there is a change, has the other one changed—or have you?

Reprinted with permission from *Celebrating Holidays* by Stacy Schumacher and Jim Fanning 1994 Twenty-Third Publications, P.O. Box 180, Mystic, CT 06355. 800-321-0411

11

Presidents' Day
Who Shall Lead Us?

On Presidents' Day we remember two of our nation's greatest leaders, George Washington and Abraham Lincoln, in one important patriotic holiday. The day can also help us Christians to reflect on God's gift of leadership and on Jesus' example of how to lead through loving service, not power. We include a fictional story of Lincoln, which, except for Molly, uses real characters and places.

Follow the Leader

Chin in hand, Molly looked up from her arithmetic book. Still chanting the five-times table, she gazed around the one-room schoolhouse. It was noisy, but Molly was used to that. Little Pigeon Creek School was a "blab school"; every boy and girl worked on their lessons out loud.

Molly's eyes flitted from the tall schoolmaster's back to the faces of her schoolmates, all busily "blabbing" their lessons, to the sunlight streaming through the long slit in the log wall that was the schoolroom's window. How she longed to be out in the sunshine and fresh air, playing the games she loved!

Then Abe, the tallest boy in the school, and the smartest, caught Molly's eye. Abe hadn't had as much schooling as some of the others, but even from across the room, Molly could hear that his reading—a story about George Washington out of Scott's Lessons in Elocution—was better than anybody else's.

Suddenly a firm, familiar voice interrupted Molly's thoughts. "Have you finished memorizing your tables, Molly?" asked Schoolmaster Dorsey. Molly was always surprised that her teacher could tell when someone stopped reciting.

"I'm up to the five-times table, Sir," replied Molly.

Schoolmaster Dorsey reached down and flipped through her text to a page full of multiplication problems. "Start ciphering those, then," he ordered, moving on to the next student.

Molly sighed. Abe would never be caught daydreaming during lessons. Abe loved to read and to learn. Every Friday afternoon the students squared off in a spelling match, and Molly knew that this Friday would be no different. Abe Lincoln would win the spelling bee, unless he secretly helped someone else win, like the day he helped Ann Roby spell "defied" by pointing to his eye.

Molly gulped as she sensed a tall presence beside her. If Schoolmaster Dorsey caught her daydreaming again . . .

"Need some help?" asked a calm, kind voice. Molly looked up and saw Abe gazing down at her and her page full of arithmetic problems. She nodded in gratitude, and Abe guided Molly through the maze of numbers until lunch time.

Outside at last, Molly thought she might finish sewing a rag doll together, which was still without a head. But she was hungry at the moment, so she fished an apple out of her lunch bucket. She heard Schoolmaster Dorsey asking Abe to lead the younger children in a game. She wasn't at all surprised that Abe chose to play Follow-the-Leader. But Molly was surprised when she saw Abe loping toward her. "These young'uns are tired of Follow-the-Leader," he said. "You're so clever at games, Molly. Can you think of something new?"

"You're good at games yourself, Abe," replied Molly, recovering as best she could from her surprise. "With those long legs of yours, you're the fastest runner in these parts."

"My tall timber legs can outrun the schoolmaster when he's after me with the switch," chuckled Abe, "but I have no head for the ins and outs of game-playing. Come on," he beckoned, starting for the children. "I know you can lead us in a game."

Molly hurried to keep up with Abe. She was already thinking how she could use her unfinished rag doll as a bean bag for a game of criss-cross catch. But she was also thinking how grand it was that Abe had turned to her for help.

Talking It Over

1. In what ways was Abe a good leader? In what way was Molly a good leader?

2. What does it mean to be a leader? What special gifts do you need to be able to guide others?

3. Can everyone be a leader in some way or another? Name some areas in which you would be a good leader.

Activity—Decoding the Message
(See page 66.)

Prayer Service—Leadership
Opening Song: "Jesus, Shepherd" by Jack Miffleton (NALR), or any suitable song.

Leader   Loving Father, you have given us your son, Jesus, to show us the path to you. In today's world Jesus works through us, his followers. Help us to follow good leaders and to lead others to you. We ask this through Christ our Lord.

All   Amen.

Leader   The Lord be with you.

All   And also with you.

Leader   A reading from the holy Gospel according to John (14:5–7)

All   Glory to you, Lord.

Reader   "Lord," said Thomas, "We do not know where you are going. How can we then know the way?" Jesus told him, "I am the way, and the truth, and the life; no one comes to the Father but through me. If you really knew me, you would know my Father also. From this point on you know him; you have seen him."
The Gospel of the Lord.

All   Praise to you, Lord Jesus Christ.

Reflections

- Ask the children what they think Jesus is teaching us in this reading. What does he mean when he says he is "the Way"? What are some of the "ways of Jesus" that the children know about?

Activity—Decoding the Message

"Common looking people are the best in the world: that is the reason the Lord makes so many of them."

Use the code below to discover a remark made by President Lincoln to his secretary, John Hay.

A = □	I = ℓ	S = .\'
B = ○	K = A	T = ≤
C = △	L = /·	W = \\'
D = ··	M = ⊙	Y = ⊓
E = ·	N = ■	
F = ⊡	O = ∴	
G = \\	P = ⊔	
H = #	R = //	

Reprinted with permission from *Celebrating Holidays* by Stacy Schumacher and Jim Fanning
1994 Twenty-Third Publications, P.O. Box 180, Mystic, CT 06355. 800-321-0411

- Jesus said that when we see him, we see the Father, but today we don't see him walking around in person. How can we see him? (in one another, in the people he sends to lead us and guide us, in the poor, in his holy word, and in the sacraments, especially the eucharist)

- Today we see Jesus with our eyes of faith, instead of with our physical eyes. But he is really with us, guiding us and leading us. When we "see" him at work in our lives, we are also seeing the Father. We "see" the Father living among us and caring for us through our parents, teachers, grandparents, and through everyone who leads us to know about God and to do good for others.

- Sometimes we follow leaders who do not walk in Jesus' footsteps. Who can think of an example? (when we join in with a "popular" kid who is making fun of someone; when we help someone cheat on a test; when we admire celebrities who take drugs; etc.) It is difficult to take a stand against these "leaders," but we can rely on Jesus to give us the strength to do it.

Litany for Leaders and Leadership

Reader 1   Our response is: Guide us, Lord Jesus.
For world leaders that they might guide their nations to peace and justice, we pray . . .

All   Guide us, Lord Jesus.

Reader 2   For our pope and all bishops, priests, and other church leaders that they might lead us to you, we pray . . .

All   Guide us, Lord Jesus.

Reader 3   For community leaders, our city government, police, and service organizations, that they might help us find ways to help one another, we pray . . .

All   Guide us, Lord Jesus.

Reader 4   For our parents, guardians, grandparents, teachers, and child care workers, that they might show us your love and teach us your paths, we pray . . .

All   Guide us, Lord Jesus.

Reader 5   That we will recognize good leaders in our friends and classmates and follow those who bring us closer to you, we pray . . .

All   Guide us, Lord Jesus.

Reader 6   That we will lead others to you through our good example and advice, we pray . . .

All Guide us, Lord Jesus.

Leader Loving Father, we thank you for your son, Jesus. Help us to follow him always. Strengthen the gifts you have given each one of us, so that we may be good leaders of those who look up to us. We ask this through our Lord Jesus Christ, who lives and reigns with you forever and ever.

All Amen.

Taking the Message Home

Who Leads Me?

Pay attention this week to those who give you advice, suggestions, or guidance. Write down their names. Circle those who you wouldn't have thought of as "leaders." Put a star next to those who are leading you along Jesus' way.

Day 1   Day 2   Day 3   Day 4   Day 5   Day 6   Day 7

_____ _____ _____ _____ _____ _____ _____

_____ _____ _____ _____ _____ _____ _____

_____ _____ _____ _____ _____ _____ _____

_____ _____ _____ _____ _____ _____ _____

_____ _____ _____ _____ _____ _____ _____

_____ _____ _____ _____ _____ _____ _____

_____ _____ _____ _____ _____ _____ _____

Thank God for all these "leaders" God has put in your life.

Reprinted with permission from *Celebrating Holidays* by Stacy Schumacher and Jim Fanning
1994 Twenty-Third Publications, P.O. Box 180, Mystic, CT 06355. 800-321-0411

Mardi Gras
Leading to Lent

Mardi Gras, French for "Fat Tuesday," is another name for Shrove Tuesday, the day before Ash Wednesday. Unfortunately, it has frequently become synonymous with excessive carnival celebrations, taking on a decidedly secular tone. Yet the idea of pre-Lenten merry-making can lead students to a more fruitful Lent, complete with prayer, almsgiving, and fasting. And preparing for Lent can bring children to a more fully celebrated Easter.

A Kid, a Coin, a Carnival

Alfredo was energetically sweeping the floor and the hot Brazilian sun lit up the dust that flew through the air. Alfredo was in a hurry to finish his daily chores, because this was the day before Ash Wednesday. The festivities of Carnival, the great celebration before the long forty days of Lent, were very much on his mind.

As more and more dust stirred, Alfredo's mother took the broom from him. "Go on," she laughed, playfully shaking the broom at her son. "You'll be no help today. Go out and see the parade."

The parade! Alfredo rushed out the door and raced down the street, anxious to find a good place to watch the magnificent procession that brought the three-day festival to an end. He couldn't wait to see the colorful banners, costumes, and headdresses. Everyone in town turned out to sing and dance in flamboyant costumes, all making merry before Lent.

Alfredo rushed past his parish church, which vaguely reminded him that he had not yet decided what he would "give up" for Lent. The thought was gone as soon as he turned the corner and saw the festive crowds lining the street. He squeezed through to get a good spot and then he waited. Finally, the parade arrived with its flower-festooned floats, the big, feathered headdresses, the glittering masks, the fancy dresses, the loud, exuberant music. Best of all, the riders on the final float tossed out "jewels," coins, and trinkets to the crowd. Alfredo eagerly reached out with all the other spectators, and to his delight, a gold coin clinked at his feet. He snatched it up and headed for home.

Alfredo looked at the shiny coin as he skipped along. He would save it for Easter and buy new clothes for himself and maybe even some candy. Suddenly, he looked up as he once more passed the church. He remembered again that he had made no special plans for Lent. Clutching his treasured coin, he pushed open the heavy door and went into the darkened church. He tiptoed up to the poor box and pushed the coin through the slot. He let out a long sigh, but then he smiled. He still wasn't sure what else he could do for Lent, but thanks to Mardi Gras, he had made a good start.

Talking It Over

1. Why do you think people celebrate just before Lent begins?

2. Why did Alfredo think it was important to do something meaningful during Lent?

3. Why do you think Alfredo gave his coin to the poor? What would you do with a gold coin? What do you think a very poor person would do with it?

Activity—Mardi Gras Masks

Dressing up is part of the festivities of Mardi Gras. Unlike Halloween, people don't try to be someone or something else. Instead, they try to look more splendid as themselves. Men and women alike use feathers, sequins, bangles, beads, satins, and velvets to make lavish outfits.

Materials needed: paper plates; yarn; hole punch; scissors; glue; an assortment of "decorations" to put on the masks—sequins, small beads, feathers, yarn, rick-rack, and cut-up construction paper pieces.

Lightly fold the paper plate in half and cut 2 eye holes on the crease. A nose and mouth can be cut by folding again but in the opposite direction, or these can be added with trimmings. Punch a hole on each edge and attach a piece of yarn to each hole. Then cover the plate with glue and add the decorations.

When the masks are completed, have a parade around the classroom or even go outside (weather permitting!). After the parade, explain that Mardi Gras is followed by Ash Wednesday, a time for prayer, fasting, and sharing.

Prayer Service—Mardi Gras

(Note: You will need diamond-shaped pieces of paper, pencils, and a basket for this prayer.)

Opening Song: "Come Along with Me to Jesus" by Carey Landry (NALR), or another suitable song.

Leader	Let us begin our prayer time together in the name of the Father, and of the Son, and of the Holy Spirit.
All	Amen.
Leader	Let us pause to think of those times when we didn't listen to Jesus' call to love. Jesus taught us to be generous, but sometimes we are selfish. Lord, have mercy.
All	Lord, have mercy.
Leader	Jesus taught us to put God first in our lives, but sometimes we think only of ourselves. Christ, have mercy.
All	Christ, have mercy.
Leader	Jesus taught us how to pray, but sometimes we forget to pray. Lord, have mercy.
All	Lord, have mercy.
Leader	May almighty God have mercy on us, forgive us our sins, and bring us to everlasting life.
All	Amen.
Leader	Let us pray. Loving creator, help us plan what we can do this Lent to get closer to you and your son, Jesus, in the power of the Holy Spirit.
All	Amen.

Leader	Mardi Gras leads to Lent. The festivities have ended and it is now time to think about God's place in our daily lives. Jesus taught us how to do this.
Reader 1	A reading from the holy Gospel according to Matthew (6:1–6, adapted) Jesus said to his followers, "Be careful that you don't do good things just to impress other people. When you give money to the poor, for example, don't make a big deal about it. Keep it to yourself and our loving God will repay you in heaven."
Reader 2	"When you pray, don't stand up in front of everybody to do it. Instead, go into a quiet place and speak to your heavenly Father and God will reward you."
Reader 3	"When you fast or give things up, don't make everyone around you think you are really suffering. Instead, do these things privately. Let it just be between you and God and you will be blessed for what you have done." The Gospel of the Lord.
All	Praise to you, Lord Jesus Christ.
Leader	Who can remember the three ways of getting close to God that Jesus just described? That's right! Prayer, fasting, and giving money to the poor. For thousands of years people have walked these three roads to God. It's easy to see how praying will bring us closer to God, but in what ways can we do this during Lent? Who has any ideas? (Daily or occasional weekday Mass, extra prayer before bed, in the morning, etc.) Fasting as a way to God is little harder to understand. Fasting means doing without, or giving up, something that we want or like. Some people give up food, snacks, chocolate, TV, or other things during Lent. Who has an idea of how this can bring us closer to God? There are two ways this works: 1) Every time we reach for or want what we have given up, we are reminded of God, for whom we are doing this. So if a person gives up desserts, he or she thinks of God at dessert time, which she or he might not have done otherwise. Fasting calls our minds to God. 2) When we feel the loss of something that we like, we can share some of the feelings of our poor brothers and sisters who do without not only extras but also things they really need. As we understand their feelings, we are even more grateful to God for all the good things we have, which we usually take for granted. What kinds of things could we fast from, or give up, this Lent? (Again, be prepared to prime the pump.) The third way we draw closer to God during Lent is by giving to the poor. This is called "almsgiving." We share what we have with

those in need because those who are in need are all brothers and sisters in the family of God. Is there some way you can earn money for the poor this Lent? To whom will you give it?

In Mardi Gras parades it is common for those on the floats to throw out gifts of jewelry to the crowd. We will write our lenten plans on these "jewels" and give them to God. List one way you will do each of the lenten practices: pray, fast, and give to the poor. (Give the children time to write their lenten plans.)

Leader Now I would like you to come forward and place your "jewels" in this basket, while I ask the Lord to bless your lenten preparations. (As each child comes forward, place your hands on his or her forehead and say, "[Name], may God bless you and help you with your lenten plans.")

Closing Song: "Jesus, Lord" by Randall DeBruyn (OCP), or another appropriate song.

Taking the Message Home

A Crown for Lent

Each time you remember to pray, fast, or save money for the poor, color one of the jewels in your lenten "crown." If Easter finds the crown brightly colored, you will have had a good Lent—and maybe, you'll have developed some new good habits!

Reprinted with permission from *Celebrating Holidays* by Stacy Schumacher and Jim Fanning
1994 Twenty-Third Publications, P.O. Box 180, Mystic, CT 06355. 800-321-0411

13

St. Patrick's Day
What's Behind the Wearin' of the Green?

In the United States and Canada, Saint Patrick's Day is celebrated with songs, parties, dances, parades, greeting cards, and the "wearin' of the green." But what's all the fuss about? Who really thinks of Saint Patrick himself on March 17th—who he was and what he has to teach us?

It's worthwhile to introduce the real Patrick, the one behind all the green drinks and leprechauns. The following fictional story about his adventures can point up some of the important truths of his life.

Patrick Finds a Way

Eighteen-year-old Patrick leaned against the trunk of a tree and looked around at the sheep. They all seemed safe, content, and busy, so he let his mind wander.

He thought about his home far away, his mother, father, and other relatives from whom he had been kidnapped three years before. He missed them very much and thought of them often as he spent long lonely days on the hillside with the sheep.

Suddenly the sun broke through the clouds lighting up the rolling green hills and sparkling on the trees and bushes, left wet by the early morning rains. "Father in heaven, the world you made is wonderful," prayed Patrick. "The Irish countryside is so pretty, it's hard to stay sad in the midst of such beauty." Patrick's gaze drifted from the hills to the sheep. Little lambs frolicked, bringing a smile to his face. "Thank you for the lambs and sheep, loving Father. They are really fun to watch. You did a good job making them!"

Then Patrick thought of Jesus who had called himself the good shepherd. He wondered if Jesus had enjoyed watching the sheep in Palestine. "Jesus," he prayed, "help me not to feel too sorry for myself, and let me remember that you, too, missed your family when you left your home to do God's work."

Plucking a shamrock from the ground, Patrick absently started chewing on the end of the stem. He had never seen shamrocks until he came to Ireland. They didn't grow in Britain, his native land. Idly, he began plucking the leaves off the stem.

Again his mind turned to prayer. "Holy Spirit, help me to continue appreciating the good things of the world, like sunshine, sheep, and shamrocks, even as I watch for a chance to escape from here. Don't let me get too discouraged with my life."

Reaching down and pulling up another shamrock, Patrick stared at the three leaves. "This reminds me of the Father, Son, and Spirit," he thought. "Three persons in one God, like the three leaves on one stem."

Patrick's prayers were interrupted by the cry of Shamus, a little lamb who was his favorite. Jumping to his feet, Patrick scanned the hillside. No sign of Shamus among all the other sheep, but he could still hear the lamb crying in the distance. Running to the top of the hill, Patrick looked out over the countryside. He now paid no attention to the sunlit beauty as he thought with rising panic, "Where is Shamus?"

Suddenly he spotted the little lamb caught in a bramble bush on the other side of the hill. Breathing a thankful prayer, Patrick dashed down the slope and freed Shamus, who bleated gratefully.

"I never knew about sheep or shamrocks until I was brought here," Patrick thought, "and I never prayed very often at home. Some good has come from the evil that happened to me. But please, heavenly Father, help me to find a way back to my family!"

Two years later, Patrick did find a way to escape, and he returned home to Britain. But he didn't forget Ireland. Many years later he returned there as a bishop, and he taught the Irish people about the Blessed Trinity, using their native shamrock as a way to explain this great mystery.

Talking It Over

1. Can you think of a time when something good came from a bad situation in your life? Did you see the good at the time, or did you only discover it later?

2. Patrick talked to God and listened to God at different times throughout the day. Do you ever do that? When do you think to pray?

3. Have you ever had to explain something difficult to someone? How did you help your listener to understand? How would you explain the Trinity to someone who had never heard this teaching?

Activity—Shamrock Suncatchers

A shamrock suncatcher can remind children of Saint Patrick's explanation of the Trinity, and it makes a nice Saint Patrick's Day decoration. Materials needed: white paper; markers or crayons; cotton balls or paper towels; vegetable oil; and construction paper strips (if you decide to frame the picture).

Have the children draw a shamrock with trim around it, or draw one yourself and make a copy for each child. Working on spread-out newspapers, put a drop of vegetable oil on each shamrock and rub the oil over the entire surface until the paper becomes opaque.

Now the shamrocks can be colored with markers or crayons. When completed, frame them with construction paper strips for a nice finished look. With or without a frame, the shamrocks can be taped in a window where the sun will shine through them.

Prayer Service—Praising the Trinity

Opening Song: "Our God Is a God of Love," by Carey Landry, or "Father, We Adore You," or another Trinitarian song.

Leader	Let us begin our prayer time in the name of the Father, and of the Son, and of the Holy Spirit.
All	Amen.
Leader	The grace of our Lord Jesus Christ, and the love of God, and the fellowship of the Holy Spirit be with you all.
All	And also with you.
Leader	Heavenly Father, you sent your Son to tell us of your love, and your Spirit to make us holy. Help us to worship you, one God in three persons, by sharing your love with others. Grant this through our Lord Jesus Christ, your Son, who lives and reigns with you and the Holy Spirit, one God, for ever and ever.

All   Amen.

Reader 1   A reading from Paul's letter to the Romans (8:14–16, adapted) Those who are led by God's Spirit are God's sons and daughters. For the Spirit that God has given us does not make us slaves or cause us to be afraid; instead, the Spirit makes us God's children. By the Spirit's power we can cry out to God, "Abba!" (which means "Father" or "Daddy"). God's Spirit joins with our spirits to say that we are God's children.
The Word of the Lord.

All   Thanks be to God.

Reader 2   Our response to the following prayers will be: Happy the people God has chosen.
The Father created the heavens by command; the sun, moon, and stars were made by God's word. When God spoke, the world was created; when God spoke, everything appeared.

All   Happy the people God has chosen.

Reader 3   The Son watches over those who trust in him. He saves them and keeps them safe in times of trouble.

All   Happy the people God has chosen.

Reader 4   We put our hope in the Holy Spirit, who is our protector and our help. May your constant love be with us, Holy Spirit, as we put our hope in you.

All   Happy the people God has chosen.

Leader   Bishop Patrick Ziemann of Santa Rosa often tells high school students that they should not pray to "God." Can you imagine why a bishop would say such a thing? The bishop tells the students that they should pray specifically to one person of the Trinity. When we pray to a person of the Trinity, we come to feel closer to that person.

When we want some help from someone in our family, we don't ask, "Family, can you help me?" No, usually we know just which one to ask for what we need. Perhaps it's best to ask your mother for money, your father for permission to spend the night at a friend's house, a brother or sister for help with math homework. (Pause here to ask the children for personal examples of this.)

With our prayers to the Trinity, the same thing is true. Each person of the Trinity shows us a different side of the love that connects them.

The Father made us and our world, protects us, and forgives us when we fail to love. Jesus, who saved us, shows us how to love the Father. He was once just your age so he knows how you feel when you are tired, scared, lonely, excited, or happy. The Spirit is within each one of us helping us to do good things, giving us strength in difficult times.

Saint Patrick explained the three persons of the Trinity to the people of Ireland, using the shamrock to show how the three were one. We cannot fully understand the Trinity, but we believe in this great mystery.

Let's take a minute now to talk to the Father, the Son, and the Spirit whose love is with us. (If your students are not familiar with meditative prayer, introduce it by saying,"This is a good way to spend time with God. It may seem strange at first, but just relax and enjoy it. Close your eyes and remain still. Try not to giggle or to distract others in any way." Then continue.)

Sit up straight in your seats. Breathe in slowly and deeply. Close your eyes. Feel the Father's love for you . . . Think of this love as a warm blanket around you. Just enjoy the Father's love for a moment . . . Now speak to Jesus in your heart. Tell him how you are feeling today . . . Tell him about the happiest or saddest thing that has happened to you recently . . . The Holy Spirit lives inside of each of us. Get in touch with the Spirit in you . . . Ask for the Spirit's help with any problem you have right now. Ask for the Spirit's strength for the hard things in your life . . .

Leader Let us now pray together. Glory be . . .

All Glory be to the Father and to the Son and to the Holy Spirit, as it was in the beginning, is now, and ever shall be, world without end. Amen.

Taking the Message Home

Shamrock Prayers

Pray to each person of the Trinity each night this week. Select a prayer or write your own.

Loving Creator, I thank you today especially for:

this wonder-full day getting through this day the pleasant weather
the much needed rain the beautiful flowers my family
for your love

Jesus, you know how I felt today when:

I got into trouble I did well in school I forgot my homework
I ate my favorite foods I felt so hungry I laughed (cried, worried, felt lonesome)
my friends got mad at me friends were there for me someone let me down

Holy Spirit, who lives within me, help me:

to be kind to my brother (sister) to obey my mother and father
to do my homework to study for my test
when I am afraid (lonely, tired) to be a good friend
to stop arguing (putting people down) to help people who need me

Reprinted with permission from *Celebrating Holidays* by Stacy Schumacher and Jim Fanning
1994 Twenty-Third Publications, P.O. Box 180, Mystic, CT 06355. 800-321-0411

14

First Day of Spring
Signs of New Life

Winter is appealing at first—cold weather and snow can be exciting. By March, however, children and adults alike are weary of winter. Our eager anticipation for spring can bring new life to the subject of baptism and Christian commitment. In the midst of the new life that surrounds us—or that we anticipate—at this time of year we remember baptismal vows and reflect on personal and earthly renewal.

A Sign for Joshua

The cold rain streaked down Josh's window like tears streaming down a face. Josh didn't feel like crying as he looked out at the storm. But he definitely felt down. He had been sick with the flu for eight long days, but now he was feeling better. His father had said last night that he could go back to school today if the weather cooperated. But naturally it was cold and rainy, so Josh had to spend one more boring day inside.

"This is supposed to be the first day of spring," Josh grumbled. "But look at that weather."

"At least it's not snowing," Josh's father said as he came into the room. Josh sighed deeply.

"I know it's hard waiting," his father continued, "but it's still too cold outside. You don't want to get sick again, do you?"

"No," replied Josh, "but I want it to be warm and sunny, like spring is supposed to be."

"It really is spring, even though we can't tell," his father said as he sat down on Josh's rumpled bed. "That's the reason—or one of the reasons—that I connect spring with new life and baptism."

"You do?" asked Josh in surprise "Why?"

"Spring has definitely sprung," his father continued. "We don't always see signs of new life, but we know they're there. When we're baptized, we begin sharing a new life, too, God's life. We've been changed, but we can't see the change."

"But there are ways we know baptism has happened," said Josh, thinking hard. "Like when we went to Kimberly's baptism last year. Aunt Sally held Kimberly and Father Joseph poured the water."

"And remember the white garment and the candle? All those things are signs—signs of God's life that Kimberly now shares."

"Even though we can't see it?" asked Josh.

"Right," answered Dad. "Luckily, we can see signs of it. And as Kim grows up, we'll start to see the most important sign of all: the way she lives her life as a member of God's family."

Josh stared thoughtfully at the soggy back yard. Through the rain-smeared window he caught a glimpse of color. Without a word, he jumped off the bed and ran down the stairs to the back door. "Dad!" he yelled. "Dad! Come quick!"

His father ran up behind him. "What is it?" he asked.

"I see a sign that spring really has sprung," said Josh, pointing toward a small yellow flower.

"It's a crocus," smiled Dad, peering through the glass.

"I'm glad it's bloomed on the first day of spring," said Josh, smiling up at his father. "I needed a sign that things really will change."

Talking It Over

1. How do you usually feel toward the end of winter? Are you ready for spring?

2. Can you think of things that spring and baptism have in common?

3. What does being baptized require of you as a child of God and follower of Jesus?

Activity—"New Life" Flower Pots

Materials needed: styrofoam cups; markers; sharp pencils; potting soil; fast-growing seeds. (Marigolds are a good choice. They grow quickly, are hardy, and can be transplanted readily.)

Have children use markers to decorate the cups with "new life" drawings, such as butterflies, eggs, flowers, candles. Poke three small holes in the bottom of the cup with the point of the pencil. Fill almost to the top with potting soil, add 2 seeds and cover lightly with soil. Remind children to water them well when they get home and continue to water them regularly in the days ahead. Encourage them to look for signs of new life in nature as they wait for their flowers to bloom.

Prayer Service—New Life

(Beforehand, gather signs or pictures of signs, as described within this service.)
Opening Song: "Signs of New Life" by Carey Landry (NALR), or another appropriate song.

Leader   Let us begin our time of prayer together in the name of the Father, and of the Son, and of the Holy Spirit.

All   Amen.

Leader   Loving creator, you gave us life and have called us to new life in your son, Jesus. Help us, through the power of the Spirit within us, to live in your love and to share it with others throughout our lives.

All   Amen.

Reader 1   Written many centuries ago, this reading describes signs of spring. Listen carefully to see if spring is the same or different today. A reading from the Song of Songs (2:11–13a): For see, the winter is past, the rains are over and gone. The flowers appear in the ground. The season of glad songs has come, the cooing of the turtledove is heard in our land. The fig tree is forming its first figs and the blossoming vines give out their fragrance.
The Word of the Lord.

All   Thanks be to God.

Leader   What signs of spring were mentioned? What are some signs of spring we see in our area? Watch and listen now as we share some of these.

Reader 2   (holding up an Easter egg, or a picture of one) An egg is as hard and cold as a tomb, but inside it can hold a new little creature. It is a sign of life.

Reader 3	(holding up a daffodil, tulip, or other bulb flower) This flower comes from a bulb, which looks as lifeless as a rock, but it holds within it the ability to produce great beauty. It is a sign of God's wonderful creation.
Reader 4	(holding up a picture of a lamb) Lambs are born in the early spring and once were offered as sacrifices to God. Today they symbolize the new life won for us by Jesus, the Lamb of God.
Reader 5	(holding up a candle) Candles chase away darkness. At our baptism we were given a candle as a sign that the Light of Christ lives in us.
Reader 6	(holding a white stole or white baptismal garment) We receive a white garment at baptism as a sign that we have put on a new life and have become a holy people.
Reader 7	(holding up a bowl of water) Water is a sign of our rebirth in Jesus' own family, with God as our loving Father. It is a sign of our call to share the message and love of Jesus with others.
Leader	We are surrounded with signs of God's love, of our relationship with God. This spring let's open our eyes and really see the signs and remember what they can mean to us. At our baptism, God's Spirit, the Holy Spirit, came to live within us. What are some of the signs in your life that you are a member of God's family? That you are filled with God's Spirit? Are there any signs of this in your homes? In your lives? In the way you act toward others? (Lead them from externals such as crucifixes, medals, rosaries, to ways of acting, such as helping others, giving to the missions, etc.)
Leader	We bless ourselves with holy water as a sign that we are baptized and are followers of Jesus. I invite you to come forward one at a time so I can bless you with holy water as a reminder of your baptism. Trace a cross on the forehead of each child as you pray, "[Name], I bless you in the name of the Father, and of the Son, and of the Holy Spirit." Invite each to answer "Amen."

Taking the Message Home

Signs of Rebirth and Renewal

A World Renewed
Circle the things you see as Earth comes to new life.

apple blossoms	birds nesting	baby lambs
rain showers	crocus	baby birds
baby chicks	lilacs	daffodils
budding trees	baby horses	butterflies
snow melting	grass sprouting	streams flowing

A Personal Renewal
Circle the things you do to show that you are born to new life in Jesus.

morning prayers	pray for brother (sister)	do homework
sort out toys	evening prayers	help teacher
read a book	work in garden	pray for parents
be cheerful	care for an animal	wash car
pray for the sick	do dishes	empty trash
clean bedroom	clean drawers	speak politely

Reprinted with permission from *Celebrating Holidays* by Stacy Schumacher and Jim Fanning 1994 Twenty-Third Publications, P.O. Box 180, Mystic, CT 06355. 800-321-0411

15

April Fool's Day
A Time for Laughter

Children love April Fool's Day, which celebrates one of God's most extravagant gifts—laughter! We find it all around us, using it in times of joy, sorrow, stress, and relaxation. Rare indeed is the person without any sense of humor. God has generously bestowed this gift on most of us.

But sometimes humor can be barbed; laughter can be at another's expense, and children can be especially cruel in using this gift. April Fool's Day is a good time to celebrate the gift and remind students that it should be used with great care.

A Lesson in Laughter

Long ago, in a kingdom on the other side of the sea, lived a clown named Harlequin. Harlequin was a happy clown who dressed in a patchwork costume of bright blues, rosy reds, and grandiose greens. On the tip of his hat and the toes of his shoes he wore little bells that jingled merrily wherever he went.

And wherever he went, people laughed and shouted, for Harlequin was the funniest clown in the land. When the brightly painted wagon he rode in arrived in a town square or village marketplace, people would forget their work and cares and come listen to Harlequin's funny stories.

After making everyone laugh, he would bow so low that the bells atop his hat would touch the dusty ground, and the delighted people would throw coins. Harlequin's boss, Sedgewick, who owned the horse-drawn wagon, greedily picked up the shiny money.

One night, as they sat by their campfire, Sedgewick said to Harlequin, "You're missing out on a chance to add more laughs to your act. Just think of all the fat and skinny people who come to see you. And what about that washerwoman who laughed so hard she dropped all her clean clothes in the street? How your audience would laugh if you made fun of those people!"

Sedgewick, you see, was greedy. He wanted more and more money, and he didn't care how he got it.

But Harlequin cared. He told Sedgewick, "People would feel bad if I made fun of them in front of their neighbors. And I want people to feel good after they see me perform!"

"I'll feel good if people give us more silver coins," bellowed Sedgewick. "So you'd better start making fun of the ugly, clumsy people in your audience!"

The clown did not answer. He went right on sewing a new patch on his costume and smiling to himself.

The next day, Harlequin and Sedgewick visited one of the largest cities in the kingdom. Hundreds of people gathered in the square to laugh at the funny clown. Sedgewick peered out of the wagon window, calculating how much money he would get from this large crowd.

Suddenly he heard Harlequin shout, "Sedgewick! I need you!" Sedgewick hurried out of the wagon. With a flourish Harlequin pointed at his boss. "Well, you react as well as a trained dog," chuckled the clown, "but you're so fat, I'm surprised you could fit through the wagon door!"

The crowd roared with laughter as Sedgewick's face turned red. He started to step down from the wagon, but he lost his footing and fell into the mud.

Over the loud laughter, Sedgewick heard Harlequin shout, "You're so graceful for one so fat! What will you do for your next trick?" Dripping with mud, Sedgewick slunk back inside the wagon.

That night, as they bumped along atop the wagon, Sedgewick was unusually quiet. Harlequin smiled mischievously. "The crowd certainly threw many coins today," he said with a twinkle in his eye. "I think I should go on being mean, don't you?"

"No, I don't," said Sedgewick. "I'm certain all those people feel very bad about their cruel laughter. We should only use laughter to help people feel good about themselves."

"What a good idea!" laughed Harlequin. "I wish I had thought of that."

Talking It Over

1. Why did Harlequin make fun of Sedgewick? Do you think he was being cruel?

2. How did Sedgewick feel when he was being made fun of? Why wasn't it worth it to him to get the extra money?

3. When you heard someone make fun of another person, how did you feel? What could you do to help in a situation like that?

Activity—April Fool Mistakes

Divide your class into teams, two students per team. Distribute the following list of religious terms and explain that some of the words are misspelled.

It's the task of each team to find the misspelled words and spell them correctly in the space next to the word. The team that finds and corrects the most mistakes wins. Give a medal to the winning team and bookmarks or holy cards to everyone else if possible. (Note: You should read through the list and discuss each word after the game.)

Biple _____

Conformation _____

Sakrament _____

Reconcilliation _____

Church _____

Altar _____

Jeses _____

Bread _____

Eucharist _____

Whine _____

Vocation _____

Marrage _____

Mass _____

Anointing _____

Priezt _____

Ordres _____

Mary _____

Absolusion _____

Preyar _____

Eastor _____

Spirit _____

Christian _____

Babtism _____

Candel _____

Prayer Service—Celebrating Laughter

Opening Song: "Joy, Joy, Joy" by Carey Landry, or "Canticle of the Sun" by Marty Haugen.

Leader	Please repeat after me: God of gifts, as we gather in your love, help us celebrate one of your greatest gifts, the gift of joy which we express in laughter. Help us make our laughter a prayerful sound pleasing to you, Lord of joy. Amen.
Reader 1	Let us now pray Psalm 100 together. Please respond: Sing with joy to the Lord!
Reader 2	Sing joyfully to the Lord all you people! Serve the Lord with gladness; come before God singing for joy.
All	Sing with joy to the Lord!
Reader 3	Know that the Lord is God who made us; we are God's people, the flock God cares for.
All	Sing with joy to the Lord!
Reader 4	Enter God's gates with thanksgiving and God's courts with songs of praise. Give thanks and bless God's name.
All	Sing with joy to the Lord!
Reader 5	The Lord's goodness and kindness last forever. God is faithful to all his people.
All	Sing with joy to the Lord!
Leader	Have you ever thought about laughter as a gift from God? Well, it is! One way we know that laughter is good and holy is that Jesus had a wonderful sense of humor. How do we know that? Well, for one thing, Jesus loved children and wherever there are children, there is laughter. Jesus also told stories when he wanted to teach. Does anyone know what these special stories are called? That's right, parables. Some of these parables were probably meant to be funny at the same time they were making a point. Remember the story of the 100 sheep from the Gospel of

Luke(15:4–7)? What happened when one of the sheep wandered off? The shepherd left the rest of the flock to look for the lost one. To Jesus' listeners, that would be a funny thing to do. Everyone knew that no shepherd would ever leave 99 sheep to go in search of one. That would be like your teacher leaving the entire class alone to go look for one student who didn't come in from the playground. The whole idea was so silly that it was funny. And yet it demonstrated to Jesus' listeners just how much God loved them.

Though Jesus may have used laughter to help people remember his stories and what he taught, he would never have used it to put people down or make them feel bad. He used laughter to help people understand God's love and enjoy God's gifts. Let's ask Jesus to help us do the same.

Reader 6	Let us now share a litany of laughter. Please respond: Lord, fill us with joy.
Reader 7	God of joy, thank you for funny stories.
All	Lord, fill us with joy.
Reader 8	God of joy, thank you for funny faces.
All	Lord, fill us with joy.
Reader 9	God of joy, thank you for funny people.
All	Lord, fill us with joy.
Reader 10	God of joy, thank you for laughter.
All	Lord, fill us with joy.
Leader	Joyful God, help us to remember that we are people of joy because we have the good news of Jesus. Help us to share this joy with everyone we meet, especially those who are sad and lonely. We ask this in the name of Jesus.
All	Amen.
Leader	As a sign of our joyful unity, let's close our prayer time by joining hands and saying together the prayer that Jesus taught us. Our Father . . .

Taking the Message Home

Looking for Good Humor

When you watch your favorite TV shows during the coming week, watch carefully! Put a check (✔) in the correct column each time the show uses "good humor": jokes that build people up and make them feel good, and each time it uses "bad humor": jokes that put people down and hurt them. Total the categories up at the end of each show.

TV Show	Good Humor	Bad Humor

Reprinted with permission from *Celebrating Holidays* by Stacy Schumacher and Jim Fanning 1994 Twenty-Third Publications, P.O. Box 180, Mystic, CT 06355. 800-321-0411

16

Earth Day
Treasuring Our Planet

Earth Day, widely celebrated in April, raises our awareness of the fragility of our planet and its environment. As Christians we are called to be good stewards of all creation. Earth Day can inspire catechists, as well as children, to better love and care for our world and all its inhabitants. A fictional story about St. Francis of Assisi, the "environmental saint," can be a focus of our discussion and prayer.

A Walk in the Woods

Giovanni looked at the dark woods surrounding him. He hadn't realized the tall trees would block out the sunlight. Glancing back at the path that disappeared into the gloom, Giovanni quickened his pace. Now he wondered if the shortcut through the forest of Assisi was such a good idea!

He tried to whistle as he peered between the dark tree trunks, but his mouth was too dry. His father would be angry if

Giovanni arrived home late, but what would his father think if he encountered a wild animal? Maybe he wouldn't get home at all!

Giovanni's thoughts were interrupted by a sound in the branches above. He drew back as he saw a large owl glaring down at him. He turned and fled deeper into the woods. Giovanni did not like the darkness of the woods or the animals that lived there. He was always glad when his father cleared away forest land to make more fields.

Breathing hard, he slowed down, then stumbled to a stop. He didn't know what to do. Just then he saw a man, slightly built and dressed in a ragged brown robe, looking at him. Giovanni knew right away that this must be the hermit, Francesco, who lived in a shack in the hills. Giovanni's father said that the hermit was crazy.

Francesco drew closer and asked, "What has caused you to flee, child?"

Giovanni drew back. "I-I saw an owl."

"Is that all?" asked Francesco, and to Giovanni's surprise, the owl fluttered down onto the hermit's outstretched arm. "You needn't fear Brother Owl."

"Owls are evil," scowled Giovanni. "They are symbols of darkness."

Francesco gently stroked the owl's feathers. "All things are created by our loving Lord and no creature of God's can be evil, except people, who sometimes choose evil."

Francesco saw that Giovanni was staring at the owl in spite of himself. "The owl is a symbol of wisdom, not evil," he said, holding the owl out to the boy. "And wisdom is knowing what our heavenly Father asks of us."

Giovanni cautiously reached out and touched the owl's feathers. "People say that you talk to the animals," he suddenly said.

Francesco laughed, and it was a kind laugh. "All of creation speaks the same language, child. All of God's creatures sing a song of harmony. We humans have to choose to join the song or disrupt it."

Giovanni smiled. "Maybe Brother Owl can help me choose the right path out of this forest. He does look like a wise old bird!"

Talking It Over

1. Francesco tells Giovanni to join the song of "harmony" of God's creatures. How can you show that you join this song?

2. Francesco, or Francis, is the patron saint of animals. He taught us to respect all animal life. How can we better respect and care for the animals God has given us?

3. Owls are a sign of wisdom. Why is it wise to take care of Earth? What are some ways you have already done this? What are some things that you might start doing?

Activity—Owl Wall Hangings

Owl hangings can remind children of their need to care for the environment. Materials needed for each child: half a sheet of construction paper; 2 small twisted pretzels; a pretzel stick; 2 elbow macaroni; 2 Cheerios; and a 20" length of yarn. Also have available a stapler, white glue, markers.

Ask the children to fold 1" of the construction paper over along the narrow edge. Put the yarn into the fold and refold two or three times. Staple the fold and tie the yarn. Glue the pretzels one above the other in the center of the paper, with the "bumpy" ends out. Glue Cheerios in the top lobes of the top pretzel. Glue the straight pretzel under the owl as a perch and add two pieces of elbow macaroni feet to complete the picture. Invite children to add sayings with markers, such as "We are wise to care for Earth," or "Give a hoot—don't pollute."

Prayer Service—Creation

Opening Song: "Thank You, Lord" by Diane Davis, or another suitable song.

Leader	The Lord be with you.
All	And also with you.
Leader	Let us pray. Lord God, you have blessed us with a beautiful world in which to live. Help us to care for this precious gift. In Jesus' name we pray.
All	Amen.
Reader 1	The response is: Blessed be God forever. Blessed are you, Lord, God of all creation. Through your goodness we have air to breathe, which keeps us healthy and helps us run and play.
All	Blessed be God forever.
Reader 2	Blessed are you, Lord, God of all creation. Through your goodness we have water to drink, which refreshes us and quenches our thirst.
All	Blessed be God forever.
Reader 3	Blessed are you, Lord, God of all creation. Through your goodness we have trees, which give us shade, provide us with food, and make oxygen for us to breathe.
All	Blessed be God forever.
Reader 4	Blessed are you, Lord, God of all creation. Through your goodness we have animals, which help us with our work, give us food, and make us happy.

All	Blessed be God forever.
Leader	Lord God, you made all good things for the good of all your people, and we give you thanks.
All	Amen.
Leader	(inviting all to stand) The Lord be with you.
All	And also with you.
Reader 5	A reading from the holy Gospel according to Luke (6:43–45) (after the reading) The Gospel of the Lord.
All	Praise to you, Lord Jesus Christ.
Leader	Close your eyes and think about these questions: • When it comes to caring for Earth, what kind of fruit do you bear? • Can others tell by the way you act that you are concerned about the environment? • In what way can you show your concerns about the environment? *(pause)* Now please repeat after me: Lord of creation, thank you for the gift of our world. Help us to protect Earth and to make every day Earth Day. We ask this through Christ our Lord. Amen.

Taking the Message Home

Save Our Earth

Do your part to save our beautiful planet. Color a leaf each time you do one of these good deeds for our Earth. Some are blank so you can fill in your own Earth-saving ideas.

17

Mother's Day
Thank God for Mothers

God gives us the gift of life through our mothers. Although abundantly aware of their mother's place in their lives, children often forget or neglect to show appreciation for all that their mothers do. Mother's Day gives them an opportunity to express their gratitude and love. It can also help to inspire them to follow her example of unselfish giving, if we point them in that direction. (Be sensitive in this celebration of those children who no longer have a mother, or are not living with their mother.)

A Bizarre Breakfast

Abby slowly pushed the door open and peered into the darkened room. "Mom?" she whispered. "We brought you something to eat."

"Come on in, Honey," said her mother in a hoarse voice from the big bed where she lay bundled up in a comforter. "I'm feeling a little better after my nap."

Abby entered her mother's room, gesturing to her brother, Wade. He struggled through the half-open door as he tried to balance a big breakfast tray. Mom cleared away a box of tissues and the old pink heating pad so Wade could set the tray down on the bed in front of her. Mom hid a smile as she looked at the lone mug in the middle of the big flat tray.

"Gee, Mom," sighed Wade, looking with disappointment at the mug full of chicken broth. "This isn't what we planned when we said we'd serve you breakfast in bed."

"Oh, Wade," snuffled Mom, propping herself up with pillows. "I appreciate your kind thoughts, but even though it's Mother's Day, I can't eat any more than this. Chicken soup has to be my breakfast in bed."

"It's not only a strange Mother's Day breakfast, but it's not even breakfast time," said Abby. "It's way past noon."

"I sure did sleep a long time! I must have needed the rest, but I'm sorry I couldn't go to Mass with you and Dad this morning," said Mom, sipping broth from the mug.

"Father Billings gave all the mothers a special blessing and we all held out our hands over them," replied Abby, sitting on the bed. "We were sorry you missed it."

"But we prayed for you anyhow," added Wade.

"We almost didn't make it ourselves," Abby continued, after nudging her brother. "Wade couldn't find his shoes and Daddy didn't know how to braid my hair."

"So I see," laughed Mom, smoothing out her daughter's hair.

"It was bad enough getting ready for church," groaned Wade. "I don't know how we'll ever get our act together for school tomorrow morning. Mom, you just have to get better!"

"Come on, now, you two are not helpless and neither is your Daddy. Our family works as a team. We all work together, we all do special things. The 'Mom' is not the most important person."

"But you do so many special things," said Abby.

"Lots more than I ever thought," chimed in Wade.

"This sounds just like at my office," said Mom, throwing up her hands. "I can't take a day off there either. But it's nice to feel appreciated, especially when I'm feeling so lousy."

"That's what Mother's Day is all about," said Wade as Mom gave both her children a hug.

"Feeling lousy?" laughed Mom.

"No, Mom, making sure you know your family appreciates you," Wade replied.

"I know you'll feel better tomorrow, Mom," said Abby, reassuringly. "And we'll celebrate Mother's Day next Sunday. We'll even ask Father Billings to give you your very own blessing."

"And if he doesn't," shrugged Wade, "we'll hold our hands out and bless you ourselves 'cause you are the world's greatest Mom!"

Talking It Over

1. Our mothers show us love in many ways. What are some ways we show our mothers that we love them? What other things could we start to do to show our mothers love?

2. Jesus calls each of us, not only mothers, to show selfless love. Who are some other people in your life who show you God's generous love by the way they live?

3. Every member of your family is important. Can you think of a time when your mother helped or contributed to you or your family? When you helped your mother or contributed to the family? When another family member went an extra mile for the good of all?

Activity—Potpourri Hearts

Have the children make their mothers a scented heart as a sign of their love—and a reminder in days to come of how sweet it is to have such a wonderful mother.

Materials needed: 2 identical 5" x 8" red, pink, or white paper hearts per child; hole punch; 3' length of red, white, or pink yarn with cellophane tape wrapped around 1 end; glue sticks; potpourri.

Have the children decorate one or both sides of the pre-cut hearts. Holding them together, they punch holes at 1" intervals around the edge. Then they run the glue stick around the bottom half of 1 heart and press them together for a minute. This prevents the potpourri from falling out. The children lace the yarn in and out of the holes, filling it with a handful of potpourri before the heart is all closed. They tie a bow at the top and take the heart home to their mothers!

Praying for Our Mothers

Opening Song: Hail Mary (sung to the tune of "Are You Sleeping")

Hail Mary,
Hail Mary,
Mother of God,
Mother of God,
The Lord is with you.
The Lord is with you.
Pray for us.
Pray for us.

Leader Today we pray to Jesus' mother, Mary, asking her to pray for our mothers. Mary knows what a hard job motherhood can be. She knows what blessings to ask the Father to give to our moms. Let us pray. Please repeat after me:

Dear Mary,
as you raised Jesus

	you trusted in the Lord God to guide you. Please pray for our mothers that the Lord's strength will be with them. Amen.
Reader 1	A reading from the holy Gospel according to Matthew (5:1–10) (after the reading) The Gospel of the Lord.
All	Praise to you, Lord Jesus Christ.
Leader	We all are called to live out these beatitudes, these guidelines to living the way Jesus wants us to. What are some ways that our mothers live them out? For example, mothers need to be "poor in spirit" when they think of their children before themselves. They are merciful over and over as their children forget to do what they are supposed to do. When you are sick or sad, your mothers suffer with you. They can be good examples of how we should all follow Jesus. We are grateful to them all year round, but we show it especially on Mother's Day. One good way to show our love is by following their examples of unselfishness.
Reader 2	We will pray a litany to Mary, our Mother in heaven. Our response is: Pray for our mothers. Mother of Jesus . . . Mother of mercy . . . Mother of faith . . .
Reader 3	Mother of wisdom . . . Mother full of grace . . . Mother of courage . . .
Reader 4	Mother of trust . . . Mother of strength . . . Mother of gentleness . . .
Reader 5	Mother of patience . . . Mother of openness . . . Mother of love . . .
Leader	Mary, you were a wonderful mother to our Lord Jesus. Pray that our mothers will be blessed as they care for us. We make this prayer in name of your son, Jesus. Amen. Closing song: "Immaculate Mary," or another suitable hymn.

Taking the Message Home

Thanking Mom More Than Once a Year

Mothers often do many, many good things for their families during a week. In the next few days, try to notice your mother doing helpful, loving things for you. Every time you catch her at it, do something nice for her—something over and above what you are normally expected to do. When you remember to do this, color a flower.

At the end of the week, present this paper to her. She will have a visible sign of your gratitude—and will know that you appreciate her!

Reprinted with permission from *Celebrating Holidays* by Stacy Schumacher and Jim Fanning 1994 Twenty-Third Publications, P.O. Box 180, Mystic, CT 06355. 800-321-0411

18
Last Day of School
A Time of Re-Creation

The last day of classes before the long summer vacation—still the norm in most school systems even though all-year schedules are making inroads—is a time of near ecstasy for most students. In the midst of all the excitement, it's a good idea to take a breather and help the children tune in to the joys of summer as a gift from God. Our creator continually re-creates us, especially in the recreational activities and fun of summertime.

Mrs. Siddle's Summer

"What's that, Marcus?" Tiffany asked her friend, pointing to the box in his hand.

"Just some candy," replied Marcus as they walked down the hall. Even though there were many other girls and boys passing by, the halls seemed empty, Tiffany thought. Not empty, bare. Everything—the posters, the students' artwork, even the teachers' memos on the big bulletin board—had been taken down. It was the last day of school and the building was ready to be closed for the summer.

"Why are you carrying around that box of candy?" Tiffany questioned her friend, above the noise of the other students.

"I brought it for Mrs. Siddle," said Marcus absently.

"Then you'd better give it to her before she's gone," Tiffany exclaimed, turning around and leading Marcus back to their classroom.

Marcus and Tiffany needn't have hurried. They found Mrs. Siddle sitting, just sitting at her desk. She turned, surprised to see the children back again after their earlier goodbyes.

"I forgot to give you this," Marcus said, thrusting the candy box at Mrs. Siddle. "I would have had to eat it myself."

"Thank you, Marcus," said Mrs. Siddle, adding the candy to the other gifts she had already placed in a cardboard box. "I don't like good-byes, but I do like good-bye gifts."

"Aren't you looking forward to the summer, Mrs. Siddle?" asked Tiffany, noticing her former teacher's downcast face.

"Well, I think I'm just having a little trouble letting go of some students I really like," answered Mrs. Siddle, smiling at the children. "But now that you've come back, I feel better. Perhaps you'd like to help me pack away the last of the school things." There were only a few piles of books, some art paper, and crayons left to be put away. Tiffany and Marcus carried these to the class cupboards and began putting them where Mrs. Siddle said they should go.

"I like summer," said Marcus as he happily hid the math books far back in the closet.

"The days are so long and the sun is so bright," said Tiffany. "And you can go swimming every day."

"And what about in religion class, when you said that all of creation is a gift from God?"

"Yeah," agreed Tiffany enthusiastically. "And what better time to enjoy God's creation?"

"I can see this teacher has a thing or two to learn," laughed Mrs. Siddle. "I like the way you give God credit for summertime."

"Of course," Tiffany stated matter-of-factly. "The beach, ice cream—God created it all."

"Just so we can have fun," chimed in Marcus, excited about all the summer promised. "And when we enjoy the summer, we enjoy God."

"A good thing too," nodded Mrs. Siddle, "because we don't want to forget God on our vacation."

"Didn't you already say that, before you gave us our report cards?" Tiffany asked.

"Am I repeating myself? Just like a teacher!"

"That's okay," Marcus said. "We don't mind listening to teachers—especially if they share their candy with their students."

"You know, I was feeling a little sad when you two came in," said Mrs. Siddle, giving her former students one last hug and extending the candy box. "But now I'm really happy about the summer!"

"Of course you are," laughed Marcus as he popped a piece of candy into his mouth. "How can anyone be sad in summer?"

Talking It Over

1. Why was Mrs. Siddle feeling a little sad? Do you ever feel that way at the end of a school year?

2. What is your favorite part of summer? What do you like most about it? How is it a gift from God?

3. Name some ways we can remember God during summer vacation.

Activity—Giant Bubble Blowing

Materials needed: large tubs, one for every 6-8 children; soapy water (use liquid dish detergent or soak scraps of soap bars in water for a few days, a thrifty way to use up something that would otherwise be wasted); various bubble blowers (1- and 2-liter soda bottles and paper cups with the bottoms cut off, plastic tubes of various sizes). If you have a very large tub, use wire coathangers formed into a circular shape.

Let the children take turns dipping blowers into the soapy water and blowing various sized bubbles. Be sure to do this on a warm day and allow extra time for damp clothing to dry.

Prayer Service—Summer Joy in the Lord

Opening Song: "Come to the Water" by John Foley, S.J., or another suitable song.

Leader	(extending one hand over a bowl of water with a small green branch in it) Loving Creator, from among the many gifts that you have given us, we celebrate today your great gift of water. We ask you to bless this water (make a cross over it), a sign of your goodness, and bless us who gather to praise you today. (Sprinkle the children with the water, shaking the excess off the branch before sprinking them.)
Reader 1	Listen to the following reading from the prophet Isaiah (55:1–3). He tells us what God promises the people. (after the reading) The Word of the Lord.
All	Thanks be to God.
Reader 2	Our response is: Give glory and praise to the Lord.
All	Give glory and praise to the Lord.
Reader 3	Bless the Lord, all you works of the Lord; praise and exalt him above all forever.
All	Give glory and praise to the Lord.
Reader 4	All you waters and seas, bless the Lord; praise and exalt him above all forever.
All	Give glory and praise to the Lord.
Reader 5	Dew and rain, bless the Lord; praise and exalt him above all forever.
All	Give glory and praise to the Lord.
Reader 6	Lightning and clouds, bless the Lord; praise and exalt him above all forever.
All	Give glory and praise to the Lord.
Reader 7	Rivers and streams, bless the Lord; praise and exalt him above all forever.
All	Give glory and praise to the Lord.
Reader 8	Dolphins and all water creatures, bless the Lord; praise and exalt him above all forever!

All	Give glory and praise to the Lord.
Reader 9	A reading from the holy Gospel according to John (7:37–38) (after the reading) The Gospel of the Lord.
All	Praise to you, Lord Jesus Christ.
Leader	What did Isaiah tell us that God will give us? (water, food, eternal life) What did Jesus say about water in John's Gospel? (he is the water, the living water) Isaiah was a prophet, one who delivered a message to us from God. Jesus was the answer to Isaiah's promise. Why did Jesus call himself "living Water"? What is there about water that tells us something about Jesus? (it is life-giving, refreshes, cleans, can bring joy and happiness) In what ways will you enjoy water this summer? Many people have fun with water during summer. As you swim, surf, fish, or splash in the months ahead, remind yourself that Jesus is our living water. When water brings you happiness, remember that he is our joy. Thinking of him when you are in or around water will help keep you close to Jesus this summer.
Reader 10	In this prayer, please respond: Refresh and renew us, O Lord. On the beach, at the lake, in rivers, and in streams . . . In pools, boats and at water parks . . . In showers and thunderstorms . . . Through flowers, birds, and trees . . . In quiet times of prayer . . . In new faces and places . . . Through those who come to us for help . . .
Leader	Let us pray. Loving creator, you have made for us a wonderful world, and in the summertime we have time to enjoy it. Help us to praise you as we relax in nature, and to remember your son, Jesus, as we play in or near the water. We pray in the name of Jesus and through the Spirit.
All	Amen.

Taking the Message Home

No Vacation From God

In the calendars below make an X each day you remember your morning prayers, a check (✔) each time you remember your evening prayers, and a happy face every time you think of Jesus when using water for summer fun.

Reprinted with permission from *Celebrating Holidays* by Stacy Schumacher and Jim Fanning
1994 Twenty-Third Publications, P.O. Box 180, Mystic, CT 06355. 800-321-0411

19

Father's Day
Thank God for Fathers

A father's love—strong, protective, caring—is a wonderful cause for celebration. Fortunate indeed is the child with such a father. Knowing that some children have fathers who are less than loving, we can still take advantage of Father's Day to celebrate good male parents, to discuss the qualities of a good father, and to thank our heavenly parent for the constant love reflected in those who care for us. (Be sensitive in this celebration of those children who no longer have a father, or are not living with their father.)

A Father's Love

Miriam dragged her water jar through the street that led to the well at the center of town. Ordinarily, she would carry the jar on her head instead of slowly dragging it across the ground. But this was no ordinary day. Her heart was as heavy as her stone water jar. She had not been near her friend's house since

Sarah had fallen into a deep, fevered sleep several days ago—the kind of sleep from which people don't wake up. Miriam could not bear to go to Sarah's house after that. The yard was full of people waiting for Sarah to die; and once she did, they started to weep and wail. Miriam hated that. How could grown-ups be so phony?

Miriam absent-mindedly drew her water jar up to the well. The water was cool and inviting, the air fresh and clear. So what? thought Miriam; there seemed to be no life without her friend.

Then, her ears picked up a strange sound. Strange because it was so familiar. A sound Miriam was sure she would never hear again.

"Miriam! I've been looking all over for you!"

Miriam turned in wonder. There, the light spring breeze blowing through her dark hair, was Sarah! She was alive!

"I love the look on your face," laughed Sarah. "You seemed so completely amazed."

"But—I thought you were . . ." gasped Miriam, unable to finish her sentence.

"I was—or so Papa says. All I remember is—well, I don't remember anything except feeling very sick. Then there was darkness, nothing."

"But how?" Miriam asked, as the two friends sat by the well.

"I heard a voice, firm but gentle, saying, 'Little girl, I say to you, arise!' Suddenly, I could open my eyes. And there was a man smiling at me. He told Papa to give me something to eat. And he was right, I was hungry!"

"I can't believe it!" said Miriam, brushing away tears. "That man must be especially blessed by God!"

"That's what Papa said," Sarah agreed. "He told me he was so afraid that I would—that I wouldn't get well, he sent for the healer everyone was talking about. And I'm so happy to see the blue sky, the beautiful flowers, my friend, and best of all," smiling broadly, "my father and his great love for me."

"Sometimes I think seeing my father's love is like seeing the face of God," said Miriam, hugging her friend.

"My father is so happy to have me well again that he gets concerned if I'm away from him too long," said Sarah, rising. "I'd better run home and show him I'm all right."

"I'll run with you," laughed Miriam, taking Sarah's hand. "Your father Jairus is so funny. I can't wait to see him joke and tease again!"

"He laughs and jokes all the time now," said Sarah, as she started off, pulling her friend with her. "It's as if he has been given a brand new life, too."

Talking It Over

1. Name some ways your father shows his love for you.

2. Jairus cared for his daughter when she was sick. Can you think of some special times when your father showed his care for you? Describe these times.

3. Sarah showed her love for Jairus by understanding his concern for her. How can you show your gratitude to your father?

4. Some children don't have fathers at home with them. Who else can care and protect like a father?

Activity—A Good Father
(See page 112.)

Prayer Service—Our Loving Father
Opening Song: "Abba Father" by Carey Landry, or another suitable song.

Leader	Let us begin our time of prayer together in the name of the Father, and of the Son, and of the Holy Spirit. Amen.
	Please repeat our opening prayer after me:
	Loving Father, you made us, you care for us, and you give us parents to love us and protect us. Bless our fathers, and all fathers all over the world. We make this prayer in the name of Jesus, our Lord and our brother. Amen.
Leader	The Lord be with you.
All	And also with you.
Leader	A reading from the holy Gospel according to Luke (8:40–42,49–56)
All	Glory to you, Lord.
Reader 1	One day a man named Jairus, a ruler of the synagogue, came up to Jesus, threw himself at Jesus' feet and begged him to come to his house because his only daughter, who was twelve, was dying. Jesus got up to go with Jairus, but on the way someone came from the ruler's house and said:

A Good Father Helps, Protects, and Loves His Child

Use the code to describe how a father might care for his children.

✝ with	🌀 helps
▢ protects	⚘ child
◊ takes	☁ during
○ homework	⊙ his
△ A father	📖 danger
⚡ of	◎ care
▽ sickness	♡ from

△ — A father 🌀 — helps
✝ — with ○ — homework

△ _____   ▢ _____

⊙ _____   ⚘ _____

♡ _____   📖 _____

△ _____   ◊ _____

◎ _____   ⚡ _____

⊙ _____   ⚘ _____

☁ _____   ▽ _____

Reprinted with permission from *Celebrating Holidays* by Stacy Schumacher and Jim Fanning
1994 Twenty-Third Publications, P.O. Box 180, Mystic, CT 06355. 800-321-0411

Reader 2	Your daughter has just died. There is no need to trouble the Master any further.
Reader 1	But Jesus said to Jairus:
Reader 3	Do not fear, just believe.
Reader 1	Jesus entered the house, taking with him only Peter, James, John, and the parents of the child. All the people were weeping and wailing loudly, so Jesus said to them:
Reader 3	Do not weep, she is not dead.
Reader 2	They laughed at Jesus, knowing that she was dead. As for Jesus, he took the child by the hand and said to her:
Reader 3	Child, awake!
Reader 2	At once her spirit returned and she got up. Then Jesus said:
Reader 3	Give her something to eat.
Reader 2	Her parents were amazed. Jesus said to them:
Reader 3	Do not let anyone know what has happened.
Leader	The Gospel of the Lord.
All	Praise to you, Lord Jesus Christ.
Leader	Jairus loved his daughter very much. What are some of the ways we can see this in the Gospel story? What are some ways your parents show that they love you very much? Can you imagine a world without parents? What would happen? Children need parents and God gives them to us—to care for us in his name. His love is shown through our parents. What are some things that loving fathers do for their children? Fathers can be powerful signs of God's loving care for us when they teach us, protect us, guide us, feed us, clothe us, shelter us. It is God's work that they are doing. Now let us thank God for the wonderful gift of fathers and ask God's blessings on our fathers, grandfathers, stepfathers, and all the men in our lives who care for us.
Reader 4	In this prayer, our response is: Heavenly Father, hear us. That our fathers will be blessed for all the good that they do for us, we pray . . .

All	Heavenly Father, hear us.
Reader 4	That all fathers will be strengthened to take good care of their children, we pray . . .
All	Heavenly Father, hear us.
Reader 5	For our grandfathers, uncles, big brothers, and stepfathers, that they will be rewarded for all the times that they have been there for us, we pray . . .
All	Heavenly Father, hear us.
Reader 5	For children without fathers or people to protect them, that church and world leaders will find ways to meet their needs, we pray . . .
All	Heavenly Father, hear us.
Reader 6	For those who are sick, especially for fathers suffering from illness, that the Lord will heal them and restore them to their families, we pray . . .
All	Heavenly Father, hear us.
Reader 7	For our own special needs that we raise to you in our hearts, we pray . . .
All	Heavenly Father, hear us.
Leader	Heavenly Father, your son, Jesus, our own brother, taught us to call you Father. We thank you for the endless love you have for each of us. When we see that love reflected through the care of our fathers and other family members, we are much blessed. Bless them with an increase of your strength and send them wonderful surprises. We make this prayer in the name of our brother, Jesus.
All	Amen.
Leader	Let us close our prayer time today by saying together the prayer that Jesus taught us. Our Father . . .

Taking the Message Home

Fathers and Father Figures—Gifts from God

Our fathers can care for us and guide us. In addition, God sends many other wonderful men into our lives—uncles, grandfathers, stepfathers, Scout leaders, teachers, and others. Write in the names of the men who help you in various ways during the week ahead, and pray for them!

| Protect | Go out with | Guide | Teach |

| Shelter | Encourage | Comfort | Tell stories |

| Play with | Advise | Feed | Correct |

Reprinted with permission from *Celebrating Holidays* by Stacy Schumacher and Jim Fanning
1994 Twenty-Third Publications, P.O. Box 180, Mystic, CT 06355. 800-321-0411

The Fourth of July
Celebrating Freedom

"The land of the free and the home of the brave" may have its problems and its ups and downs, but it is much blessed. Citizens of the United States enjoy so many freedoms not available in other lands that it seems natural for us to take them for granted. As we celebrate our nation's birth, we can contemplate God's bountiful blessings on our country—and renew our commitment to use our gifts for the good of all.

Excitement at the Inn

Nat looked worriedly at the large, black horse he led toward the stable. "Come on, Ebony," coaxed Nat. He was anxious to get the exhausted horse settled; he had the other horses to think of. Nat was the stable boy of the Spotted Dog Inn, located in Philadelphia between Carpenter's Hall and Independence Hall, where important meetings were going on daily in the Second Continental Congress. It was Nat's job to care for the horses of the inn's many guests. Tonight the Spotted Dog was packed—people filled all the beds, and horses jammed the stable. Tomorrow morning the most important session of all would take place, a large gathering of the most important people in the colonies.

But Nat knew he must focus on his job. Ebony needed him and other mounts were waiting. He led the sweat-drenched horse into a stall and began brushing him, talking calmly and slowly. "You had a long ride, didn't you, boy?" Ebony looked at the boy with his big brown and seemingly grateful eyes.

Nat carefully placed a blanket over his friend. It was always hot in Philadelphia in summer, but this July seemed especially humid, partly explaining Ebony's overheated condition. The main reason was that Ebony had just carried Charles Carroll, a member of the Continental Congress, on part of his journey from Canada. Mr. Carroll had been in Canada trying to enlist that country's help in the colonies' fight for independence. He had failed in that mission, but wanting to be in Philadelphia in time to vote for the Declaration of Independence, Mr. Carroll had ridden night and day to get there on time.

Nat was fascinated by such delegates as Ben Franklin, John Adams, and Thomas Jefferson and often lingered in the inn's courtyard to overhear their conversations. But he was most interested in Mr. Carroll. Nat was a Catholic and so was Mr. Carroll. Nat knew from his own experience that Catholics were often made fun of in the American colonies. Mr. Carroll wanted to vote for America's freedom because the new country would be based on freedom, a gift from God. He hoped, and Nat did too, that religious freedom would make life easier for the Catholic citizens.

"You did good, boy," Nat whispered to Ebony, who felt cooler and calmer. Once he made sure all the horses had enough hay, Nat headed through the inn and across the cobblestone streets. Maybe he could stop at Independence Hall and listen in as Mr. Jefferson's Declaration of Independence was debated one last time for final changes. Nat hurried along, thinking he could perhaps even catch a glimpse of Mr. Carroll getting ready to sign the Declaration.

But first Nat planned to stop by at his church for a moment and pray—for Mr. Carroll, for the Continental Congress, for himself, for Ebony, for all of the new nation born of God's great gift of freedom.

Nat looked up into the heavens as he strode along; the starred sky seemed filled with glory to celebrate the approaching freedom of the colonies. Nat felt in his heart that the Fourth of July, 1776, was a date he'd remember for the rest of his life.

Talking It Over

1. Nat knew the importance of freedom, since he himself had suffered discrimination because of his religion. How have you learned to appreciate your freedoms? Are there some rights you take for granted?

2. In his own small way, Nat helped the cause of freedom. Have you ever had an opportunity to lend a hand in an important matter?

3. Charles Carroll gave up the comfort of his own home and rode without sleep to be a part of the Continental Congress's vote on the Declaration of Independence. Have you ever been so dedicated to a cause? What cause can you think of that could make you drop everything to work on it?

Activity—A "Fourth" Crossword
(See page 119.)

Prayer Service—Let Freedom Ring
Opening Song: "America the Beautiful," or another suitable song.

Leader   We pray together today in the name of the Father, and of the Son, and of the Holy Spirit.

All   Amen.

Leader   Let us pray. Gracious God, you have given us the wonderful gift of freedom, so that we can freely choose to respond to your love. Keep us close to you always and help us to know your will so that we can choose wisely and well. We ask this through Christ our Lord.

All   Amen.

Reader 1   A reading from the book of Exodus (19:2–7, adapted) After Moses led the Israelites out of Egypt, where they were held captive, he went up a mountain and God spoke to him: "You have seen how I led you and your people out of the land of slavery to freedom. If you listen to me and keep our covenant, you shall all be my special possession, a holy nation." When Moses told the people what God had said, they all shouted, "Everything that God has said, we shall do." The Word of the Lord.

All   Thanks be to God.

Reader 1   Our response is: Our God is a God of freedom.

A "Fourth" Crossword Puzzle

This crossword puzzle is different than most others—wherever you would write the letters for our country's birthday, write the numeral instead. To give you the idea, #14 across is done for you.

ACROSS
3. Luckily
4. Ahead or in front of
8. Always
9. From another country
10. A pattern, shape
12. Good or bad luck
13. Pardon, reconcile
14. The ___ of July
16. Wager
17. Something to eat with
18. The day you were born
20. An adult female
21. Pass out cards
22. An American car company

DOWN
1. Round handle
2. Secure place for an army
3. Surrender, give up
5. Strength, power
6. Something to write with
7. Many trees
8. Can't remember
9. The top of your face
10. False, counterfeit
11. A baseball glove
13. Prohibit, ban
14. Number of dimes in $4
15. A group of cows
17. A very fancy dress or dance
18. Not good
19. Can pay for

All	Our God is a God of freedom.
Reader 2	From flood, God delivered Noah and his family.
All	Our God is a God of freedom.
Reader 3	From famine, God delivered Jacob and his sons.
All	Our God is a God of freedom.
Reader 4	From slavery, God delivered Moses and the Israelites.
All	Our God is a God of freedom.
Reader 5	From Goliath and the Philistines, God delivered David.
All	Our God is a God of freedom.
Reader 6	From captivity in Babylon, God delivered the people.
All	Our God is a God of freedom.
Reader 7	From slavery to sin, Jesus has delivered us all.
All	Our God is a God of freedom.
Reader 8	From all that is evil, God delivers us.
All	Our God is a God of freedom.
Leader	We are so blessed to be in this country of freedom. Do you know of any ways that you are free that boys and girls in other countries are not? (to worship as we choose, to vote for our leaders, to move about at will, to say what we want, to read newspapers) Many people do not have the kind of freedom we have; many come to this country seeking freedom. Did anyone here come from another country? Do you know anyone who did? Why did they come here? Since we have so much freedom here in the United States, sometimes we take it for granted. We forget to be grateful. Let us pray now in thanksgiving for what we have and ask God's help for those who lack liberty. Our response is: Lord, hear our prayer.
Reader 1	For those unable to worship you freely and openly, we pray . . .
All	Lord, hear our prayer.

Reader 2	For children who must work for food and are not free to go to school, we pray . . .
All	Lord, hear our prayer.
Reader 3	For people who live under dictators and have no choice in their political leaders, we pray . . .
All	Lord, hear our prayer.
Reader 4	For those unable to own land, homes, or the means to provide for themselves and their families, we pray . . .
All	Lord, hear our prayer.
Reader 5	For those held back by government repression, we pray . . .
All	Lord, hear our prayer.
Reader 6	For the hungry and homeless whose poverty keeps them from enjoying the fruits of freedom, we pray . . .
All	Lord, hear our prayer.
Reader 7	For the sick and the dying, that God will free them from their suffering, we pray . . .
All	Lord, hear our prayer.
Reader 8	That we who have much will find ways to help those who are not free, we pray . . .
All	Lord, hear our prayer.
Leader	God of freedom, you have saved your people over and over and led us to true freedom in your son, Jesus. Help us to appreciate the freedom we enjoy and to work to bring freedom to those who are enslaved. We pray with confidence that you will hear and answer us.
All	Amen.

Taking the Message Home

How Many Ways Am I Free?

1. Free to eat what I want
2. Free to play
3. Free to read
4. Free to pray
5. Free to choose my friends
6. Free to study and learn
7. Free to watch TV
8. Free to travel
9. Free to shop
10. Free to say what I want
11. Free to dress as I please
12. Free to _____

For each day, write the numbers of the freedoms you use. For #12, write the word for the other freedom you experience.

Day 1_____

Day 2 _____

Day 3_____

Day 4 _____

Day 5_____

Day 6 _____

Day 7_____

Thank you, Lord, for my freedom. Help me to use it well to do your will.

Puzzle Solutions

Page 29

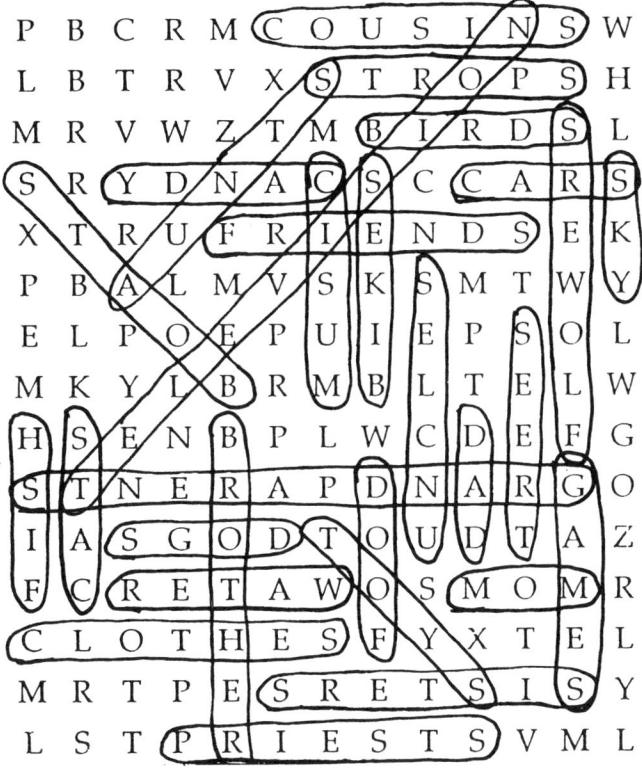

Page 54
"Deep in our hearts we do believe we shall overcome some day."

Page 66
"Common-looking people are the best in the world; that is the reason the Lord makes so many of them."

Page 89

Biple	Bible	Mass	
Conformation	Confirmation	Anointing	
Sakrament	Sacrament	Priezt	Priest
Reconcilliation	Reconciliation	Ordres	Orders
Church		Mary	
Altar		Absolusion	Absolution
Jeses	Jesus	Preyar	Prayer
Bread		Eastor	Easter
Eucharist		Spirit	
Whine	Wine	Christian	
Vocation		Babtism	Baptism
Marrage	Marriage	Candel	Candle

123

Page 112

A father protects his child from danger.
A father helps with homework.
A father takes care of his child during sickness.

Page 119

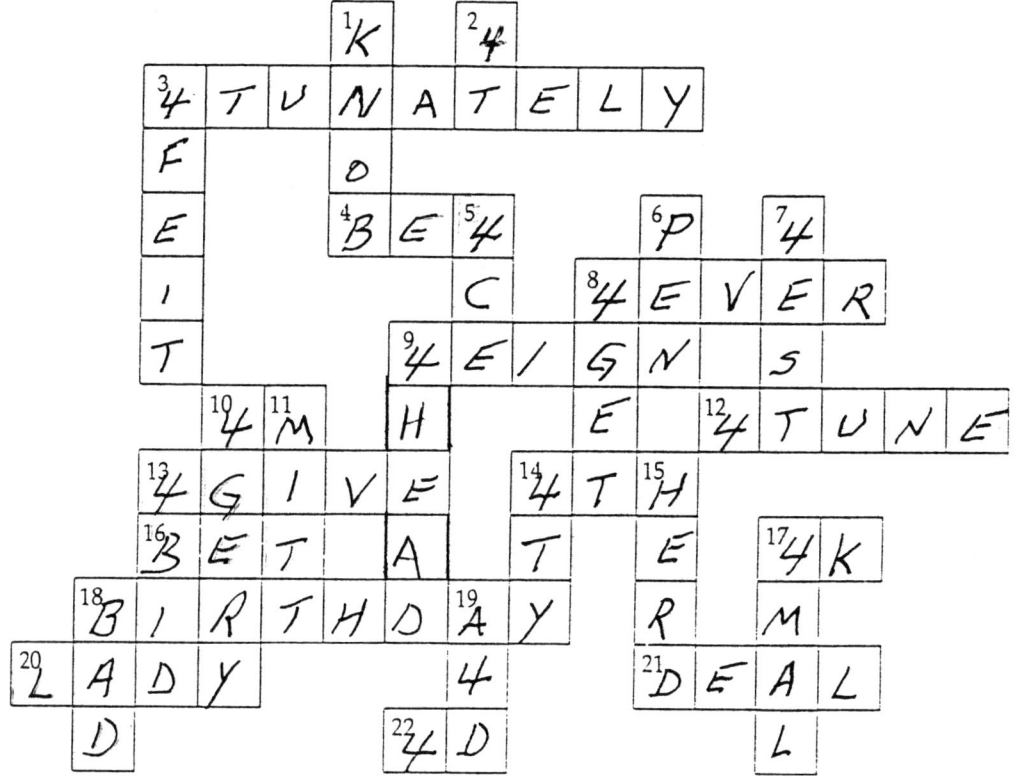

Of Related Interest...

Learning by Doing
150 Activities to Enrich Religion Classes for Young Children
Carole MacClennan
A systematic yet simple "lesson wheel" approach where the lesson is seen as a wheel with a hub (topic) that is connected by spokes (sensory activities designed to engage the attention of young children) to the rim (completed objectives).
ISBN: 0-89622-562-3, 128 pp, $14.95

When Jesus Was Young
Carole MacClennan
Helps children in grades K-5 understand the life and times of Jesus through activities such as grinding wheat for bread or weaving a mat.
ISBN: 0-89622-485-6, 80 pp, $7.95

Leading Students Into Prayer
Ideas and Suggestions from A to Z
Sr. Mary Kathleen Glavich
Explores the varied forms that prayer takes, along with tips on how to teach these techniques to children.
ISBN: 0-89622-549-6, 160 pp, $12.95

Prayer Services for Young Children
30 Ten-Minute Celebrations
Gayle Schreiber
This resource involves preschool and primary grade students in brief prayer experiences that follow themes such as belonging, families, creation, holy days, holidays and saints' days.
ISBN: 0-89622-542-9, 72 pp, $9.95

Seasonal Prayer Services for Teenagers
Greg Dues
This collection of 16 prayer services helps teenagers understand the themes found in the holidays of the seasons, the church year and the civic year.
ISBN: 0-89622-473-2, 80 pp, $9.95

Available at religious bookstores or from
TWENTY-THIRD PUBLICATIONS
P.O. Box 180 • Mystic, CT 06355
1-800-321-0411